Saint's Divine Intercessory Prayers

Ruby W. Smith, B.S., M.S., N.D.

authorHOUSE®

AuthorHouse™
1663 Liberty Drive
Bloomington, IN 47403
www.authorhouse.com
Phone: 1 (800) 839-8640

Published by AuthorHouse 04/29/2015

ISBN: 978-1-5049-0979-2 (sc)
ISBN: 978-1-5049-0980-8 (e)

Library of Congress Control Number: 2015906761

Print information available on the last page.

KJV
Scripture quotations marked KJV are from the Holy Bible, King James Version (Authorized Version). First published in 1611. Quoted from the KJV Classic Reference Bible, Copyright © 1983 by The Zondervan Corporation.

Contents

PREFACE

Dear Journal Writer,

I was inspired my Lord to create this journal. The journal is to help you monitor the intercessory prayers you pray for others. I will help you have a closer walk with God, as you study the Word and apply it to your prayer life.

To intercede for others demonstrates love, and it is one of the most rewarding, personal, and spiritual experiences you can share. The Lord hears sincere and unselfish prayers and He honors them.

I pray that you will be a blessing to others and be blessed by using the journal, "Saint's Divine Intercessory Prayers."

R. W. S.

PRAYER NEED

_____

_____

_____

Scripture

_____

_____

_____

Date Prayer Answered/Confirmed

_____

_____

_____

PRAYER NEED

_____

_____

_____

Scripture

_____

_____

_____

Date Prayer Answered/Confirmed

_____

_____

_____

PRAYER NEED

_____

_____

_____

Scripture

_____

_____

_____

Date Prayer Answered/Confirmed

_____

_____

_____

PRAYER NEED

_____

_____

_____

Scripture

_____

_____

_____

Date Prayer Answered/Confirmed

_____

_____

_____

PRAYER NEED

_____

_____

_____

Scripture

_____

_____

_____

Date Prayer Answered/Confirmed

_____

_____

_____

PRAYER NEED

_____

_____

_____

Scripture

_____

_____

_____

Date Prayer Answered/Confirmed

_____

_____

_____

Ruby W. Smith, B.S., M.S., N.D.

PRAYER NEED

_____

_____

_____

Scripture

_____

_____

_____

Date Prayer Answered/Confirmed

_____

_____

_____

PRAYER NEED

_____

_____

_____

Scripture

_____

_____

_____

Date Prayer Answered/Confirmed

_____

_____

_____

PRAYER NEED

_____

_____

_____

Scripture

_____

_____

_____

Date Prayer Answered/Confirmed

_____

_____

_____

PRAYER NEED

_____

_____

_____

Scripture

_____

_____

_____

Date Prayer Answered/Confirmed

_____

_____

_____

PRAYER NEED

_____

_____

_____

Scripture

_____

_____

_____

Date Prayer Answered/Confirmed

_____

_____

_____

PRAYER NEED

_____

_____

_____

Scripture

_____

_____

_____

Date Prayer Answered/Confirmed

_____

_____

_____

PRAYER NEED

_____

_____

_____

Scripture

_____

_____

_____

Date Prayer Answered/Confirmed

_____

_____

_____

PRAYER NEED

_____

_____

_____

Scripture

_____

_____

_____

Date Prayer Answered/Confirmed

_____

_____

_____

PRAYER NEED

_____

_____

_____

Scripture

_____

_____

_____

Date Prayer Answered/Confirmed

_____

_____

_____

PRAYER NEED

_____

_____

_____

Scripture

_____

_____

_____

Date Prayer Answered/Confirmed

_____

_____

_____

PRAYER NEED

_____
_____
_____

Scripture

_____
_____
_____

Date Prayer Answered/Confirmed

_____
_____
_____

PRAYER NEED

_____
_____
_____

Scripture

_____
_____
_____

Date Prayer Answered/Confirmed

_____
_____
_____

PRAYER NEED

_____
_____
_____

Scripture

_____
_____
_____

Date Prayer Answered/Confirmed

_____
_____
_____

PRAYER NEED

_____
_____
_____

Scripture

_____
_____
_____

Date Prayer Answered/Confirmed

_____
_____
_____

PRAYER NEED

_____

_____

_____

Scripture

_____

_____

_____

Date Prayer Answered/Confirmed

_____

_____

_____

PRAYER NEED

_____

_____

_____

Scripture

_____

_____

_____

Date Prayer Answered/Confirmed

_____

_____

_____

Ruby W. Smith, B.S., M.S., N.D.

PRAYER NEED

_____

_____

_____

Scripture

_____

_____

_____

Date Prayer Answered/Confirmed

_____

_____

_____

PRAYER NEED

_____

_____

_____

Scripture

_____

_____

_____

Date Prayer Answered/Confirmed

_____

_____

_____

PRAYER NEED

_____
_____
_____

Scripture

_____
_____
_____

Date Prayer Answered/Confirmed

_____
_____
_____

PRAYER NEED

_____
_____
_____

Scripture

_____
_____
_____

Date Prayer Answered/Confirmed

_____
_____
_____

PRAYER NEED

_____

_____

_____

Scripture

_____

_____

_____

Date Prayer Answered/Confirmed

_____

_____

_____

PRAYER NEED

_____

_____

_____

Scripture

_____

_____

_____

Date Prayer Answered/Confirmed

_____

_____

_____

PRAYER NEED

_____

_____

_____

Scripture

_____

_____

_____

Date Prayer Answered/Confirmed

_____

_____

_____

PRAYER NEED

_____

_____

_____

Scripture

_____

_____

_____

Date Prayer Answered/Confirmed

_____

_____

_____

PRAYER NEED

_____

_____

_____

Scripture

_____

_____

_____

Date Prayer Answered/Confirmed

_____

_____

_____

PRAYER NEED

_____

_____

_____

Scripture

_____

_____

_____

Date Prayer Answered/Confirmed

_____

_____

_____

PRAYER NEED

_____

_____

_____

Scripture

_____

_____

_____

Date Prayer Answered/Confirmed

_____

_____

_____

PRAYER NEED

_____

_____

_____

Scripture

_____

_____

_____

Date Prayer Answered/Confirmed

_____

_____

_____

PRAYER NEED

_____

_____

_____

Scripture

_____

_____

_____

Date Prayer Answered/Confirmed

_____

_____

_____

PRAYER NEED

_____

_____

_____

Scripture

_____

_____

_____

Date Prayer Answered/Confirmed

_____

_____

_____

PRAYER NEED

_____

_____

_____

Scripture

_____

_____

_____

Date Prayer Answered/Confirmed

_____

_____

_____

PRAYER NEED

_____

_____

_____

Scripture

_____

_____

_____

Date Prayer Answered/Confirmed

_____

_____

_____

PRAYER NEED

_____

_____

_____

Scripture

_____

_____

_____

Date Prayer Answered/Confirmed

_____

_____

_____

PRAYER NEED

_____

_____

_____

Scripture

_____

_____

_____

Date Prayer Answered/Confirmed

_____

_____

_____

PRAYER NEED

_____

_____

_____

Scripture

_____

_____

_____

Date Prayer Answered/Confirmed

_____

_____

_____

PRAYER NEED

_____

_____

_____

Scripture

_____

_____

_____

Date Prayer Answered/Confirmed

_____

_____

_____

PRAYER NEED

_____

_____

_____

Scripture

_____

_____

_____

Date Prayer Answered/Confirmed

_____

_____

_____

PRAYER NEED

_____

_____

_____

Scripture

_____

_____

_____

Date Prayer Answered/Confirmed

_____

_____

_____

PRAYER NEED

_____

_____

_____

Scripture

_____

_____

_____

Date Prayer Answered/Confirmed

_____

_____

_____

PRAYER NEED

_____

_____

_____

Scripture

_____

_____

_____

Date Prayer Answered/Confirmed

_____

_____

_____

PRAYER NEED

_____

_____

_____

Scripture

_____

_____

_____

Date Prayer Answered/Confirmed

_____

_____

_____

PRAYER NEED

_____

_____

_____

Scripture

_____

_____

_____

Date Prayer Answered/Confirmed

_____

_____

_____

PRAYER NEED

_____

_____

_____

Scripture

_____

_____

_____

Date Prayer Answered/Confirmed

_____

_____

_____

PRAYER NEED

_____

_____

_____

Scripture

_____

_____

_____

Date Prayer Answered/Confirmed

_____

_____

_____

PRAYER NEED

_____

_____

_____

Scripture

_____

_____

_____

Date Prayer Answered/Confirmed

_____

_____

_____

PRAYER NEED

_____

_____

_____

Scripture

_____

_____

_____

Date Prayer Answered/Confirmed

_____

_____

_____

PRAYER NEED

_____
_____
_____

Scripture

_____
_____
_____

Date Prayer Answered/Confirmed

_____
_____
_____

PRAYER NEED

_____
_____
_____

Scripture

_____
_____
_____

Date Prayer Answered/Confirmed

_____
_____
_____

PRAYER NEED

_____

_____

_____

Scripture

_____

_____

_____

Date Prayer Answered/Confirmed

_____

_____

_____

PRAYER NEED

_____

_____

_____

Scripture

_____

_____

_____

Date Prayer Answered/Confirmed

_____

_____

_____

PRAYER NEED

_____

_____

_____

Scripture

_____

_____

_____

Date Prayer Answered/Confirmed

_____

_____

_____

PRAYER NEED

_____

_____

_____

Scripture

_____

_____

_____

Date Prayer Answered/Confirmed

_____

_____

_____

Ruby W. Smith, B.S., M.S., N.D.

PRAYER NEED

_____

_____

_____

Scripture

_____

_____

_____

Date Prayer Answered/Confirmed

_____

_____

_____

PRAYER NEED

_____

_____

_____

Scripture

_____

_____

_____

Date Prayer Answered/Confirmed

_____

_____

_____

PRAYER NEED

_____

_____

_____

Scripture

_____

_____

_____

Date Prayer Answered/Confirmed

_____

_____

_____

PRAYER NEED

_____

_____

_____

Scripture

_____

_____

_____

Date Prayer Answered/Confirmed

_____

_____

_____

Ruby W. Smith, B.S., M.S., N.D.

PRAYER NEED

_____

_____

_____

Scripture

_____

_____

_____

Date Prayer Answered/Confirmed

_____

_____

_____

PRAYER NEED

_____

_____

_____

Scripture

_____

_____

_____

Date Prayer Answered/Confirmed

_____

_____

_____

PRAYER NEED

_____

_____

_____

Scripture

_____

_____

_____

Date Prayer Answered/Confirmed

_____

_____

_____

PRAYER NEED

_____

_____

_____

Scripture

_____

_____

_____

Date Prayer Answered/Confirmed

_____

_____

_____

PRAYER NEED

_____

_____

_____

Scripture

_____

_____

_____

Date Prayer Answered/Confirmed

_____

_____

_____

PRAYER NEED

_____

_____

_____

Scripture

_____

_____

_____

Date Prayer Answered/Confirmed

_____

_____

_____

PRAYER NEED

_____

_____

_____

Scripture

_____

_____

_____

Date Prayer Answered/Confirmed

_____

_____

_____

PRAYER NEED

_____

_____

_____

Scripture

_____

_____

_____

Date Prayer Answered/Confirmed

_____

_____

_____

PRAYER NEED

_____

_____

_____

Scripture

_____

_____

_____

Date Prayer Answered/Confirmed

_____

_____

_____

PRAYER NEED

_____

_____

_____

Scripture

_____

_____

_____

Date Prayer Answered/Confirmed

_____

_____

_____

PRAYER NEED

_____

_____

_____

Scripture

_____

_____

_____

Date Prayer Answered/Confirmed

_____

_____

_____

PRAYER NEED

_____

_____

_____

Scripture

_____

_____

_____

Date Prayer Answered/Confirmed

_____

_____

_____

PRAYER NEED

_____

_____

_____

Scripture

_____

_____

_____

Date Prayer Answered/Confirmed

_____

_____

_____

PRAYER NEED

_____

_____

_____

Scripture

_____

_____

_____

Date Prayer Answered/Confirmed

_____

_____

_____

PRAYER NEED

_____

_____

_____

Scripture

_____

_____

_____

Date Prayer Answered/Confirmed

_____

_____

_____

PRAYER NEED

_____

_____

_____

Scripture

_____

_____

_____

Date Prayer Answered/Confirmed

_____

_____

_____

PRAYER NEED

_____

_____

_____

Scripture

_____

_____

_____

Date Prayer Answered/Confirmed

_____

_____

_____

PRAYER NEED

_____

_____

_____

Scripture

_____

_____

_____

Date Prayer Answered/Confirmed

_____

_____

_____

PRAYER NEED

_____
_____
_____

Scripture

_____
_____
_____

Date Prayer Answered/Confirmed

_____
_____
_____

PRAYER NEED

_____
_____
_____

Scripture

_____
_____
_____

Date Prayer Answered/Confirmed

_____
_____
_____

PRAYER NEED

_____

_____

_____

Scripture

_____

_____

_____

Date Prayer Answered/Confirmed

_____

_____

_____

PRAYER NEED

_____

_____

_____

Scripture

_____

_____

_____

Date Prayer Answered/Confirmed

_____

_____

_____

PRAYER NEED

_____

_____

_____

Scripture

_____

_____

_____

Date Prayer Answered/Confirmed

_____

_____

_____

PRAYER NEED

_____

_____

_____

Scripture

_____

_____

_____

Date Prayer Answered/Confirmed

_____

_____

_____

Ruby W. Smith, B.S., M.S., N.D.

PRAYER NEED

_____

_____

_____

Scripture

_____

_____

_____

Date Prayer Answered/Confirmed

_____

_____

_____

PRAYER NEED

_____

_____

_____

Scripture

_____

_____

_____

Date Prayer Answered/Confirmed

_____

_____

_____

PRAYER NEED

_____

_____

_____

Scripture

_____

_____

_____

Date Prayer Answered/Confirmed

_____

_____

_____

PRAYER NEED

_____

_____

_____

Scripture

_____

_____

_____

Date Prayer Answered/Confirmed

_____

_____

_____

PRAYER NEED

_____

_____

_____

Scripture

_____

_____

_____

Date Prayer Answered/Confirmed

_____

_____

_____

PRAYER NEED

_____

_____

_____

Scripture

_____

_____

_____

Date Prayer Answered/Confirmed

_____

_____

_____

PRAYER NEED

_____

_____

_____

Scripture

_____

_____

_____

Date Prayer Answered/Confirmed

_____

_____

_____

PRAYER NEED

_____

_____

_____

Scripture

_____

_____

_____

Date Prayer Answered/Confirmed

_____

_____

_____

PRAYER NEED

_____

_____

_____

Scripture

_____

_____

_____

Date Prayer Answered/Confirmed

_____

_____

_____

PRAYER NEED

_____

_____

_____

Scripture

_____

_____

_____

Date Prayer Answered/Confirmed

_____

_____

_____

PRAYER NEED

_____

_____

_____

Scripture

_____

_____

_____

Date Prayer Answered/Confirmed

_____

_____

_____

PRAYER NEED

_____

_____

_____

Scripture

_____

_____

_____

Date Prayer Answered/Confirmed

_____

_____

_____

PRAYER NEED

_____
_____
_____

Scripture

_____
_____
_____

Date Prayer Answered/Confirmed

_____
_____
_____

PRAYER NEED

_____
_____
_____

Scripture

_____
_____
_____

Date Prayer Answered/Confirmed

_____
_____
_____

PRAYER NEED

_____

_____

_____

Scripture

_____

_____

_____

Date Prayer Answered/Confirmed

_____

_____

_____

PRAYER NEED

_____

_____

_____

Scripture

_____

_____

_____

Date Prayer Answered/Confirmed

_____

_____

_____

PRAYER NEED

_____

_____

_____

Scripture

_____

_____

_____

Date Prayer Answered/Confirmed

_____

_____

_____

PRAYER NEED

_____

_____

_____

Scripture

_____

_____

_____

Date Prayer Answered/Confirmed

_____

_____

_____

PRAYER NEED

_____

_____

_____

Scripture

_____

_____

_____

Date Prayer Answered/Confirmed

_____

_____

_____

PRAYER NEED

_____

_____

_____

Scripture

_____

_____

_____

Date Prayer Answered/Confirmed

_____

_____

_____

Ruby W. Smith, B.S., M.S., N.D.

PRAYER NEED

_____

_____

_____

Scripture

_____

_____

_____

Date Prayer Answered/Confirmed

_____

_____

_____

PRAYER NEED

_____

_____

_____

Scripture

_____

_____

_____

Date Prayer Answered/Confirmed

_____

_____

_____

PRAYER NEED

_____

_____

_____

Scripture

_____

_____

_____

Date Prayer Answered/Confirmed

_____

_____

_____

PRAYER NEED

_____

_____

_____

Scripture

_____

_____

_____

Date Prayer Answered/Confirmed

_____

_____

_____

Ruby W. Smith, B.S., M.S., N.D.

PRAYER NEED

_____

_____

_____

Scripture

_____

_____

_____

Date Prayer Answered/Confirmed

_____

_____

_____

PRAYER NEED

_____

_____

_____

Scripture

_____

_____

_____

Date Prayer Answered/Confirmed

_____

_____

_____

PRAYER NEED

_____
_____
_____

Scripture

_____
_____
_____

Date Prayer Answered/Confirmed

_____
_____
_____

PRAYER NEED

_____
_____
_____

Scripture

_____
_____
_____

Date Prayer Answered/Confirmed

_____
_____
_____

PRAYER NEED

_____

_____

_____

Scripture

_____

_____

_____

Date Prayer Answered/Confirmed

_____

_____

_____

PRAYER NEED

_____

_____

_____

Scripture

_____

_____

_____

Date Prayer Answered/Confirmed

_____

_____

_____

PRAYER NEED

_____

_____

_____

Scripture

_____

_____

_____

Date Prayer Answered/Confirmed

_____

_____

_____

PRAYER NEED

_____

_____

_____

Scripture

_____

_____

_____

Date Prayer Answered/Confirmed

_____

_____

_____

PRAYER NEED

_____

_____

_____

Scripture

_____

_____

_____

Date Prayer Answered/Confirmed

_____

_____

_____

PRAYER NEED

_____

_____

_____

Scripture

_____

_____

_____

Date Prayer Answered/Confirmed

_____

_____

_____

PRAYER NEED

_____

_____

_____

Scripture

_____

_____

_____

Date Prayer Answered/Confirmed

_____

_____

_____

PRAYER NEED

_____

_____

_____

Scripture

_____

_____

_____

Date Prayer Answered/Confirmed

_____

_____

_____

PRAYER NEED

_____

_____

_____

Scripture

_____

_____

_____

Date Prayer Answered/Confirmed

_____

_____

_____

PRAYER NEED

_____

_____

_____

Scripture

_____

_____

_____

Date Prayer Answered/Confirmed

_____

_____

_____

PRAYER NEED

_____

_____

_____

Scripture

_____

_____

_____

Date Prayer Answered/Confirmed

_____

_____

_____

PRAYER NEED

_____

_____

_____

Scripture

_____

_____

_____

Date Prayer Answered/Confirmed

_____

_____

_____

Ruby W. Smith, B.S., M.S., N.D.

PRAYER NEED

_____

_____

_____

Scripture

_____

_____

_____

Date Prayer Answered/Confirmed

_____

_____

_____

PRAYER NEED

_____

_____

_____

Scripture

_____

_____

_____

Date Prayer Answered/Confirmed

_____

_____

_____

PRAYER NEED

_____

_____

_____

Scripture

_____

_____

_____

Date Prayer Answered/Confirmed

_____

_____

_____

PRAYER NEED

_____

_____

_____

Scripture

_____

_____

_____

Date Prayer Answered/Confirmed

_____

_____

_____

PRAYER NEED

_____

_____

_____

Scripture

_____

_____

_____

Date Prayer Answered/Confirmed

_____

_____

_____

PRAYER NEED

_____

_____

_____

Scripture

_____

_____

_____

Date Prayer Answered/Confirmed

_____

_____

_____

PRAYER NEED

_____

_____

_____

Scripture

_____

_____

_____

Date Prayer Answered/Confirmed

_____

_____

_____

PRAYER NEED

_____

_____

_____

Scripture

_____

_____

_____

Date Prayer Answered/Confirmed

_____

_____

_____

Ruby W. Smith, B.S., M.S., N.D.

PRAYER NEED

_____

_____

_____

Scripture

_____

_____

_____

Date Prayer Answered/Confirmed

_____

_____

_____

PRAYER NEED

_____

_____

_____

Scripture

_____

_____

_____

Date Prayer Answered/Confirmed

_____

_____

_____

PRAYER NEED

_____

_____

_____

Scripture

_____

_____

_____

Date Prayer Answered/Confirmed

_____

_____

_____

PRAYER NEED

_____

_____

_____

Scripture

_____

_____

_____

Date Prayer Answered/Confirmed

_____

_____

_____

Ruby W. Smith, B.S., M.S., N.D.

PRAYER NEED

_____

_____

_____

Scripture

_____

_____

_____

Date Prayer Answered/Confirmed

_____

_____

_____

PRAYER NEED

_____

_____

_____

Scripture

_____

_____

_____

Date Prayer Answered/Confirmed

_____

_____

_____

PRAYER NEED

_____

_____

_____

Scripture

_____

_____

_____

Date Prayer Answered/Confirmed

_____

_____

_____

PRAYER NEED

_____

_____

_____

Scripture

_____

_____

_____

Date Prayer Answered/Confirmed

_____

_____

_____

PRAYER NEED

_____

_____

_____

Scripture

_____

_____

_____

Date Prayer Answered/Confirmed

_____

_____

_____

PRAYER NEED

_____

_____

_____

Scripture

_____

_____

_____

Date Prayer Answered/Confirmed

_____

_____

_____

PRAYER NEED

_____

_____

_____

Scripture

_____

_____

_____

Date Prayer Answered/Confirmed

_____

_____

_____

PRAYER NEED

_____

_____

_____

Scripture

_____

_____

_____

Date Prayer Answered/Confirmed

_____

_____

_____

Ruby W. Smith, B.S., M.S., N.D.

PRAYER NEED

_____

_____

_____

Scripture

_____

_____

_____

Date Prayer Answered/Confirmed

_____

_____

_____

PRAYER NEED

_____

_____

_____

Scripture

_____

_____

_____

Date Prayer Answered/Confirmed

_____

_____

_____

PRAYER NEED

_____

_____

_____

Scripture

_____

_____

_____

Date Prayer Answered/Confirmed

_____

_____

_____

PRAYER NEED

_____

_____

_____

Scripture

_____

_____

_____

Date Prayer Answered/Confirmed

_____

_____

_____

Ruby W. Smith, B.S., M.S., N.D.

PRAYER NEED

_____

_____

_____

Scripture

_____

_____

_____

Date Prayer Answered/Confirmed

_____

_____

_____

PRAYER NEED

_____

_____

_____

Scripture

_____

_____

_____

Date Prayer Answered/Confirmed

_____

_____

_____

PRAYER NEED

_____

_____

_____

Scripture

_____

_____

_____

Date Prayer Answered/Confirmed

_____

_____

_____

PRAYER NEED

_____

_____

_____

Scripture

_____

_____

_____

Date Prayer Answered/Confirmed

_____

_____

_____

PRAYER NEED

_____

_____

_____

Scripture

_____

_____

_____

Date Prayer Answered/Confirmed

_____

_____

_____

PRAYER NEED

_____

_____

_____

Scripture

_____

_____

_____

Date Prayer Answered/Confirmed

_____

_____

_____

PRAYER NEED

_____

_____

_____

Scripture

_____

_____

_____

Date Prayer Answered/Confirmed

_____

_____

_____

PRAYER NEED

_____

_____

_____

Scripture

_____

_____

_____

Date Prayer Answered/Confirmed

_____

_____

_____

Ruby W. Smith, B.S., M.S., N.D.

PRAYER NEED

_____
_____
_____

Scripture

_____
_____
_____

Date Prayer Answered/Confirmed

_____
_____
_____

PRAYER NEED

_____
_____
_____

Scripture

_____
_____
_____

Date Prayer Answered/Confirmed

_____
_____
_____

PRAYER NEED

_____

_____

_____

Scripture

_____

_____

_____

Date Prayer Answered/Confirmed

_____

_____

_____

PRAYER NEED

_____

_____

_____

Scripture

_____

_____

_____

Date Prayer Answered/Confirmed

_____

_____

_____

Ruby W. Smith, B.S., M.S., N.D.

PRAYER NEED

_____

_____

_____

Scripture

_____

_____

_____

Date Prayer Answered/Confirmed

_____

_____

_____

PRAYER NEED

_____

_____

_____

Scripture

_____

_____

_____

Date Prayer Answered/Confirmed

_____

_____

_____

PRAYER NEED

_____

_____

_____

Scripture

_____

_____

_____

Date Prayer Answered/Confirmed

_____

_____

_____

PRAYER NEED

_____

_____

_____

Scripture

_____

_____

_____

Date Prayer Answered/Confirmed

_____

_____

_____

PRAYER NEED

_____

_____

_____

Scripture

_____

_____

_____

Date Prayer Answered/Confirmed

_____

_____

_____

PRAYER NEED

_____

_____

_____

Scripture

_____

_____

_____

Date Prayer Answered/Confirmed

_____

_____

_____

PRAYER NEED

_____

_____

_____

Scripture

_____

_____

_____

Date Prayer Answered/Confirmed

_____

_____

_____

PRAYER NEED

_____

_____

_____

Scripture

_____

_____

_____

Date Prayer Answered/Confirmed

_____

_____

_____

PRAYER NEED

_____

_____

_____

Scripture

_____

_____

_____

Date Prayer Answered/Confirmed

_____

_____

_____

PRAYER NEED

_____

_____

_____

Scripture

_____

_____

_____

Date Prayer Answered/Confirmed

_____

_____

_____

PRAYER NEED

_____

_____

_____

Scripture

_____

_____

_____

Date Prayer Answered/Confirmed

_____

_____

_____

PRAYER NEED

_____

_____

_____

Scripture

_____

_____

_____

Date Prayer Answered/Confirmed

_____

_____

_____

PRAYER NEED

_____

_____

_____

Scripture

_____

_____

_____

Date Prayer Answered/Confirmed

_____

_____

_____

PRAYER NEED

_____

_____

_____

Scripture

_____

_____

_____

Date Prayer Answered/Confirmed

_____

_____

_____

PRAYER NEED

_____

_____

_____

Scripture

_____

_____

_____

Date Prayer Answered/Confirmed

_____

_____

_____

PRAYER NEED

_____

_____

_____

Scripture

_____

_____

_____

Date Prayer Answered/Confirmed

_____

_____

_____

Ruby W. Smith, B.S., M.S., N.D.

PRAYER NEED

_____

_____

_____

Scripture

_____

_____

_____

Date Prayer Answered/Confirmed

_____

_____

_____

PRAYER NEED

_____

_____

_____

Scripture

_____

_____

_____

Date Prayer Answered/Confirmed

_____

_____

_____

PRAYER NEED

_____

_____

_____

Scripture

_____

_____

_____

Date Prayer Answered/Confirmed

_____

_____

_____

PRAYER NEED

_____

_____

_____

Scripture

_____

_____

_____

Date Prayer Answered/Confirmed

_____

_____

_____

PRAYER NEED

_____

_____

_____

Scripture

_____

_____

_____

Date Prayer Answered/Confirmed

_____

_____

_____

PRAYER NEED

_____

_____

_____

Scripture

_____

_____

_____

Date Prayer Answered/Confirmed

_____

_____

_____

PRAYER NEED

_____
_____
_____

Scripture

_____
_____
_____

Date Prayer Answered/Confirmed

_____
_____
_____

PRAYER NEED

_____
_____
_____

Scripture

_____
_____
_____

Date Prayer Answered/Confirmed

_____
_____
_____

PRAYER NEED

_____

_____

_____

Scripture

_____

_____

_____

Date Prayer Answered/Confirmed

_____

_____

_____

PRAYER NEED

_____

_____

_____

Scripture

_____

_____

_____

Date Prayer Answered/Confirmed

_____

_____

_____

PRAYER NEED

_____

_____

_____

Scripture

_____

_____

_____

Date Prayer Answered/Confirmed

_____

_____

_____

PRAYER NEED

_____

_____

_____

Scripture

_____

_____

_____

Date Prayer Answered/Confirmed

_____

_____

_____

Ruby W. Smith, B.S., M.S., N.D.

PRAYER NEED

_____

_____

_____

Scripture

_____

_____

_____

Date Prayer Answered/Confirmed

_____

_____

_____

PRAYER NEED

_____

_____

_____

Scripture

_____

_____

_____

Date Prayer Answered/Confirmed

_____

_____

_____

PRAYER NEED

_____

_____

_____

Scripture

_____

_____

_____

Date Prayer Answered/Confirmed

_____

_____

_____

PRAYER NEED

_____

_____

_____

Scripture

_____

_____

_____

Date Prayer Answered/Confirmed

_____

_____

_____

PRAYER NEED

_____

_____

_____

Scripture

_____

_____

_____

Date Prayer Answered/Confirmed

_____

_____

_____

PRAYER NEED

_____

_____

_____

Scripture

_____

_____

_____

Date Prayer Answered/Confirmed

_____

_____

_____

PRAYER NEED

_____

_____

_____

Scripture

_____

_____

_____

Date Prayer Answered/Confirmed

_____

_____

_____

PRAYER NEED

_____

_____

_____

Scripture

_____

_____

_____

Date Prayer Answered/Confirmed

_____

_____

_____

PRAYER NEED

_____

_____

_____

Scripture

_____

_____

_____

Date Prayer Answered/Confirmed

_____

_____

_____

PRAYER NEED

_____

_____

_____

Scripture

_____

_____

_____

Date Prayer Answered/Confirmed

_____

_____

_____

PRAYER NEED

_____

_____

_____

Scripture

_____

_____

_____

Date Prayer Answered/Confirmed

_____

_____

_____

PRAYER NEED

_____

_____

_____

Scripture

_____

_____

_____

Date Prayer Answered/Confirmed

_____

_____

_____

PRAYER NEED

_____

_____

_____

Scripture

_____

_____

_____

Date Prayer Answered/Confirmed

_____

_____

_____

PRAYER NEED

_____

_____

_____

Scripture

_____

_____

_____

Date Prayer Answered/Confirmed

_____

_____

_____

PRAYER NEED

_____

_____

_____

Scripture

_____

_____

_____

Date Prayer Answered/Confirmed

_____

_____

_____

PRAYER NEED

_____

_____

_____

Scripture

_____

_____

_____

Date Prayer Answered/Confirmed

_____

_____

_____

Ruby W. Smith, B.S., M.S., N.D.

PRAYER NEED

_____

_____

_____

Scripture

_____

_____

_____

Date Prayer Answered/Confirmed

_____

_____

_____

PRAYER NEED

_____

_____

_____

Scripture

_____

_____

_____

Date Prayer Answered/Confirmed

_____

_____

_____

PRAYER NEED

_____
_____
_____

Scripture

_____
_____
_____

Date Prayer Answered/Confirmed

_____
_____
_____

PRAYER NEED

_____
_____
_____

Scripture

_____
_____
_____

Date Prayer Answered/Confirmed

_____
_____
_____

PRAYER NEED

_____

_____

_____

Scripture

_____

_____

_____

Date Prayer Answered/Confirmed

_____

_____

_____

PRAYER NEED

_____

_____

_____

Scripture

_____

_____

_____

Date Prayer Answered/Confirmed

_____

_____

_____

PRAYER NEED

_____

_____

_____

Scripture

_____

_____

_____

Date Prayer Answered/Confirmed

_____

_____

_____

PRAYER NEED

_____

_____

_____

Scripture

_____

_____

_____

Date Prayer Answered/Confirmed

_____

_____

_____

Ruby W. Smith, B.S., M.S., N.D.

PRAYER NEED

_____

_____

_____

Scripture

_____

_____

_____

Date Prayer Answered/Confirmed

_____

_____

_____

PRAYER NEED

_____

_____

_____

Scripture

_____

_____

_____

Date Prayer Answered/Confirmed

_____

_____

_____

PRAYER NEED

_____
_____
_____

Scripture

_____
_____
_____

Date Prayer Answered/Confirmed

_____
_____
_____

PRAYER NEED

_____
_____
_____

Scripture

_____
_____
_____

Date Prayer Answered/Confirmed

_____
_____
_____

Ruby W. Smith, B.S., M.S., N.D.

PRAYER NEED

_____

_____

_____

Scripture

_____

_____

_____

Date Prayer Answered/Confirmed

_____

_____

_____

PRAYER NEED

_____

_____

_____

Scripture

_____

_____

_____

Date Prayer Answered/Confirmed

_____

_____

_____

PRAYER NEED

_____

_____

_____

Scripture

_____

_____

_____

Date Prayer Answered/Confirmed

_____

_____

_____

PRAYER NEED

_____

_____

_____

Scripture

_____

_____

_____

Date Prayer Answered/Confirmed

_____

_____

_____

Ruby W. Smith, B.S., M.S., N.D.

PRAYER NEED

_____

_____

_____

Scripture

_____

_____

_____

Date Prayer Answered/Confirmed

_____

_____

_____

PRAYER NEED

_____

_____

_____

Scripture

_____

_____

_____

Date Prayer Answered/Confirmed

_____

_____

_____

PRAYER NEED

_____

_____

_____

Scripture

_____

_____

_____

Date Prayer Answered/Confirmed

_____

_____

_____

PRAYER NEED

_____

_____

_____

Scripture

_____

_____

_____

Date Prayer Answered/Confirmed

_____

_____

_____

PRAYER NEED

_____

_____

_____

Scripture

_____

_____

_____

Date Prayer Answered/Confirmed

_____

_____

_____

PRAYER NEED

_____

_____

_____

Scripture

_____

_____

_____

Date Prayer Answered/Confirmed

_____

_____

_____

PRAYER NEED

_____

_____

_____

Scripture

_____

_____

_____

Date Prayer Answered/Confirmed

_____

_____

_____

PRAYER NEED

_____

_____

_____

Scripture

_____

_____

_____

Date Prayer Answered/Confirmed

_____

_____

_____

PRAYER NEED

_____

_____

_____

Scripture

_____

_____

_____

Date Prayer Answered/Confirmed

_____

_____

_____

PRAYER NEED

_____

_____

_____

Scripture

_____

_____

_____

Date Prayer Answered/Confirmed

_____

_____

_____

PRAYER NEED

_____

_____

_____

Scripture

_____

_____

_____

Date Prayer Answered/Confirmed

_____

_____

_____

PRAYER NEED

_____

_____

_____

Scripture

_____

_____

_____

Date Prayer Answered/Confirmed

_____

_____

_____

PRAYER NEED

_____

_____

_____

Scripture

_____

_____

_____

Date Prayer Answered/Confirmed

_____

_____

_____

PRAYER NEED

_____

_____

_____

Scripture

_____

_____

_____

Date Prayer Answered/Confirmed

_____

_____

_____

PRAYER NEED

_____

_____

_____

Scripture

_____

_____

_____

Date Prayer Answered/Confirmed

_____

_____

_____

PRAYER NEED

_____

_____

_____

Scripture

_____

_____

_____

Date Prayer Answered/Confirmed

_____

_____

_____

PRAYER NEED

_____

_____

_____

Scripture

_____

_____

_____

Date Prayer Answered/Confirmed

_____

_____

_____

PRAYER NEED

_____

_____

_____

Scripture

_____

_____

_____

Date Prayer Answered/Confirmed

_____

_____

_____

PRAYER NEED

_____

_____

_____

Scripture

_____

_____

_____

Date Prayer Answered/Confirmed

_____

_____

_____

PRAYER NEED

_____

_____

_____

Scripture

_____

_____

_____

Date Prayer Answered/Confirmed

_____

_____

_____

PRAYER NEED

_____

_____

_____

Scripture

_____

_____

_____

Date Prayer Answered/Confirmed

_____

_____

_____

PRAYER NEED

_____

_____

_____

Scripture

_____

_____

_____

Date Prayer Answered/Confirmed

_____

_____

_____

PRAYER NEED

_____

_____

_____

Scripture

_____

_____

_____

Date Prayer Answered/Confirmed

_____

_____

_____

PRAYER NEED

_____

_____

_____

Scripture

_____

_____

_____

Date Prayer Answered/Confirmed

_____

_____

_____

PRAYER NEED

_____

_____

_____

Scripture

_____

_____

_____

Date Prayer Answered/Confirmed

_____

_____

_____

PRAYER NEED

_____

_____

_____

Scripture

_____

_____

_____

Date Prayer Answered/Confirmed

_____

_____

_____

PRAYER NEED

_____

_____

_____

Scripture

_____

_____

_____

Date Prayer Answered/Confirmed

_____

_____

_____

PRAYER NEED

_____

_____

_____

Scripture

_____

_____

_____

Date Prayer Answered/Confirmed

_____

_____

_____

Ruby W. Smith, B.S., M.S., N.D.

PRAYER NEED

_____

_____

_____

Scripture

_____

_____

_____

Date Prayer Answered/Confirmed

_____

_____

_____

PRAYER NEED

_____

_____

_____

Scripture

_____

_____

_____

Date Prayer Answered/Confirmed

_____

_____

_____

126

PRAYER NEED

_____

_____

_____

Scripture

_____

_____

_____

Date Prayer Answered/Confirmed

_____

_____

_____

PRAYER NEED

_____

_____

_____

Scripture

_____

_____

_____

Date Prayer Answered/Confirmed

_____

_____

_____

PRAYER NEED

_____

_____

_____

Scripture

_____

_____

_____

Date Prayer Answered/Confirmed

_____

_____

_____

PRAYER NEED

_____

_____

_____

Scripture

_____

_____

_____

Date Prayer Answered/Confirmed

_____

_____

_____

PRAYER NEED

_____

_____

_____

Scripture

_____

_____

_____

Date Prayer Answered/Confirmed

_____

_____

_____

PRAYER NEED

_____

_____

_____

Scripture

_____

_____

_____

Date Prayer Answered/Confirmed

_____

_____

_____

PRAYER NEED

_____

_____

_____

Scripture

_____

_____

_____

Date Prayer Answered/Confirmed

_____

_____

_____

PRAYER NEED

_____

_____

_____

Scripture

_____

_____

_____

Date Prayer Answered/Confirmed

_____

_____

_____

PRAYER NEED

_____
_____
_____

Scripture

_____
_____
_____

Date Prayer Answered/Confirmed

_____
_____
_____

PRAYER NEED

_____
_____
_____

Scripture

_____
_____
_____

Date Prayer Answered/Confirmed

_____
_____
_____

Ruby W. Smith, B.S., M.S., N.D.

PRAYER NEED

_____

_____

_____

Scripture

_____

_____

_____

Date Prayer Answered/Confirmed

_____

_____

_____

PRAYER NEED

_____

_____

_____

Scripture

_____

_____

_____

Date Prayer Answered/Confirmed

_____

_____

_____

PRAYER NEED

_____

_____

_____

Scripture

_____

_____

_____

Date Prayer Answered/Confirmed

_____

_____

_____

PRAYER NEED

_____

_____

_____

Scripture

_____

_____

_____

Date Prayer Answered/Confirmed

_____

_____

_____

Ruby W. Smith, B.S., M.S., N.D.

PRAYER NEED

_____

_____

_____

Scripture

_____

_____

_____

Date Prayer Answered/Confirmed

_____

_____

_____

PRAYER NEED

_____

_____

_____

Scripture

_____

_____

_____

Date Prayer Answered/Confirmed

_____

_____

_____

PRAYER NEED

_____

_____

_____

Scripture

_____

_____

_____

Date Prayer Answered/Confirmed

_____

_____

_____

PRAYER NEED

_____

_____

_____

Scripture

_____

_____

_____

Date Prayer Answered/Confirmed

_____

_____

_____

PRAYER NEED

_____

_____

_____

Scripture

_____

_____

_____

Date Prayer Answered/Confirmed

_____

_____

_____

PRAYER NEED

_____

_____

_____

Scripture

_____

_____

_____

Date Prayer Answered/Confirmed

_____

_____

_____

PRAYER NEED

_____

_____

_____

Scripture

_____

_____

_____

Date Prayer Answered/Confirmed

_____

_____

_____

PRAYER NEED

_____

_____

_____

Scripture

_____

_____

_____

Date Prayer Answered/Confirmed

_____

_____

_____

Ruby W. Smith, B.S., M.S., N.D.

PRAYER NEED

_____

_____

_____

Scripture

_____

_____

_____

Date Prayer Answered/Confirmed

_____

_____

_____

PRAYER NEED

_____

_____

_____

Scripture

_____

_____

_____

Date Prayer Answered/Confirmed

_____

_____

_____

PRAYER NEED

_____
_____
_____

Scripture

_____
_____
_____

Date Prayer Answered/Confirmed

_____
_____
_____

PRAYER NEED

_____
_____
_____

Scripture

_____
_____
_____

Date Prayer Answered/Confirmed

_____
_____
_____

PRAYER NEED

_____

_____

_____

Scripture

_____

_____

_____

Date Prayer Answered/Confirmed

_____

_____

_____

PRAYER NEED

_____

_____

_____

Scripture

_____

_____

_____

Date Prayer Answered/Confirmed

_____

_____

_____

PRAYER NEED

_____

_____

_____

Scripture

_____

_____

_____

Date Prayer Answered/Confirmed

_____

_____

_____

PRAYER NEED

_____

_____

_____

Scripture

_____

_____

_____

Date Prayer Answered/Confirmed

_____

_____

_____

PRAYER NEED

_____

_____

_____

Scripture

_____

_____

_____

Date Prayer Answered/Confirmed

_____

_____

_____

PRAYER NEED

_____

_____

_____

Scripture

_____

_____

_____

Date Prayer Answered/Confirmed

_____

_____

_____

PRAYER NEED

_____

_____

_____

Scripture

_____

_____

_____

Date Prayer Answered/Confirmed

_____

_____

_____

PRAYER NEED

_____

_____

_____

Scripture

_____

_____

_____

Date Prayer Answered/Confirmed

_____

_____

_____

PRAYER NEED

_____

_____

_____

Scripture

_____

_____

_____

Date Prayer Answered/Confirmed

_____

_____

_____

PRAYER NEED

_____

_____

_____

Scripture

_____

_____

_____

Date Prayer Answered/Confirmed

_____

_____

_____

PRAYER NEED

_____

_____

_____

Scripture

_____

_____

_____

Date Prayer Answered/Confirmed

_____

_____

_____

PRAYER NEED

_____

_____

_____

Scripture

_____

_____

_____

Date Prayer Answered/Confirmed

_____

_____

_____

PRAYER NEED

_____

_____

_____

Scripture

_____

_____

_____

Date Prayer Answered/Confirmed

_____

_____

_____

PRAYER NEED

_____

_____

_____

Scripture

_____

_____

_____

Date Prayer Answered/Confirmed

_____

_____

_____

PRAYER NEED

_____

_____

_____

Scripture

_____

_____

_____

Date Prayer Answered/Confirmed

_____

_____

_____

PRAYER NEED

_____

_____

_____

Scripture

_____

_____

_____

Date Prayer Answered/Confirmed

_____

_____

_____

PRAYER NEED

_____

_____

_____

Scripture

_____

_____

_____

Date Prayer Answered/Confirmed

_____

_____

_____

PRAYER NEED

_____

_____

_____

Scripture

_____

_____

_____

Date Prayer Answered/Confirmed

_____

_____

_____

PRAYER NEED

_____

_____

_____

Scripture

_____

_____

_____

Date Prayer Answered/Confirmed

_____

_____

_____

PRAYER NEED

_____

_____

_____

Scripture

_____

_____

_____

Date Prayer Answered/Confirmed

_____

_____

_____

Ruby W. Smith, B.S., M.S., N.D.

PRAYER NEED

_____

_____

_____

Scripture

_____

_____

_____

Date Prayer Answered/Confirmed

_____

_____

_____

PRAYER NEED

_____

_____

_____

Scripture

_____

_____

_____

Date Prayer Answered/Confirmed

_____

_____

_____

PRAYER NEED

_____

_____

_____

Scripture

_____

_____

_____

Date Prayer Answered/Confirmed

_____

_____

_____

PRAYER NEED

_____

_____

_____

Scripture

_____

_____

_____

Date Prayer Answered/Confirmed

_____

_____

_____

Ruby W. Smith, B.S., M.S., N.D.

PRAYER NEED

_____

_____

_____

Scripture

_____

_____

_____

Date Prayer Answered/Confirmed

_____

_____

_____

PRAYER NEED

_____

_____

_____

Scripture

_____

_____

_____

Date Prayer Answered/Confirmed

_____

_____

_____

PRAYER NEED

_____

_____

_____

Scripture

_____

_____

_____

Date Prayer Answered/Confirmed

_____

_____

_____

PRAYER NEED

_____

_____

_____

Scripture

_____

_____

_____

Date Prayer Answered/Confirmed

_____

_____

_____

Ruby W. Smith, B.S., M.S., N.D.

PRAYER NEED

_____

_____

_____

Scripture

_____

_____

_____

Date Prayer Answered/Confirmed

_____

_____

_____

PRAYER NEED

_____

_____

_____

Scripture

_____

_____

_____

Date Prayer Answered/Confirmed

_____

_____

_____

PRAYER NEED

_____

_____

_____

Scripture

_____

_____

_____

Date Prayer Answered/Confirmed

_____

_____

_____

PRAYER NEED

_____

_____

_____

Scripture

_____

_____

_____

Date Prayer Answered/Confirmed

_____

_____

_____

Ruby W. Smith, B.S., M.S., N.D.

PRAYER NEED

_____

_____

_____

Scripture

_____

_____

_____

Date Prayer Answered/Confirmed

_____

_____

_____

PRAYER NEED

_____

_____

_____

Scripture

_____

_____

_____

Date Prayer Answered/Confirmed

_____

_____

_____

PRAYER NEED

_____

_____

_____

Scripture

_____

_____

_____

Date Prayer Answered/Confirmed

_____

_____

_____

PRAYER NEED

_____

_____

_____

Scripture

_____

_____

_____

Date Prayer Answered/Confirmed

_____

_____

_____

Ruby W. Smith, B.S., M.S., N.D.

PRAYER NEED

_____

_____

_____

Scripture

_____

_____

_____

Date Prayer Answered/Confirmed

_____

_____

_____

PRAYER NEED

_____

_____

_____

Scripture

_____

_____

_____

Date Prayer Answered/Confirmed

_____

_____

_____

PRAYER NEED

_____

_____

_____

Scripture

_____

_____

_____

Date Prayer Answered/Confirmed

_____

_____

_____

PRAYER NEED

_____

_____

_____

Scripture

_____

_____

_____

Date Prayer Answered/Confirmed

_____

_____

_____

Ruby W. Smith, B.S., M.S., N.D.

PRAYER NEED

_____

_____

_____

Scripture

_____

_____

_____

Date Prayer Answered/Confirmed

_____

_____

_____

PRAYER NEED

_____

_____

_____

Scripture

_____

_____

_____

Date Prayer Answered/Confirmed

_____

_____

_____

PRAYER NEED

_____

_____

_____

Scripture

_____

_____

_____

Date Prayer Answered/Confirmed

_____

_____

_____

PRAYER NEED

_____

_____

_____

Scripture

_____

_____

_____

Date Prayer Answered/Confirmed

_____

_____

_____

Ruby W. Smith, B.S., M.S., N.D.

PRAYER NEED

_____

_____

_____

Scripture

_____

_____

_____

Date Prayer Answered/Confirmed

_____

_____

_____

PRAYER NEED

_____

_____

_____

Scripture

_____

_____

_____

Date Prayer Answered/Confirmed

_____

_____

_____

PRAYER NEED

_____

_____

_____

Scripture

_____

_____

_____

Date Prayer Answered/Confirmed

_____

_____

_____

PRAYER NEED

_____

_____

_____

Scripture

_____

_____

_____

Date Prayer Answered/Confirmed

_____

_____

_____

PRAYER NEED

_____

_____

_____

Scripture

_____

_____

_____

Date Prayer Answered/Confirmed

_____

_____

_____

PRAYER NEED

_____

_____

_____

Scripture

_____

_____

_____

Date Prayer Answered/Confirmed

_____

_____

_____

PRAYER NEED

_____

_____

_____

Scripture

_____

_____

_____

Date Prayer Answered/Confirmed

_____

_____

_____

PRAYER NEED

_____

_____

_____

Scripture

_____

_____

_____

Date Prayer Answered/Confirmed

_____

_____

_____

Ruby W. Smith, B.S., M.S., N.D.

PRAYER NEED

_____

_____

_____

Scripture

_____

_____

_____

Date Prayer Answered/Confirmed

_____

_____

_____

PRAYER NEED

_____

_____

_____

Scripture

_____

_____

_____

Date Prayer Answered/Confirmed

_____

_____

_____

PRAYER NEED

_____

_____

_____

Scripture

_____

_____

_____

Date Prayer Answered/Confirmed

_____

_____

_____

PRAYER NEED

_____

_____

_____

Scripture

_____

_____

_____

Date Prayer Answered/Confirmed

_____

_____

_____

Ruby W. Smith, B.S., M.S., N.D.

PRAYER NEED

_____

_____

_____

Scripture

_____

_____

_____

Date Prayer Answered/Confirmed

_____

_____

_____

PRAYER NEED

_____

_____

_____

Scripture

_____

_____

_____

Date Prayer Answered/Confirmed

_____

_____

_____

PRAYER NEED

_____

_____

_____

Scripture

_____

_____

_____

Date Prayer Answered/Confirmed

_____

_____

_____

PRAYER NEED

_____

_____

_____

Scripture

_____

_____

_____

Date Prayer Answered/Confirmed

_____

_____

_____

PRAYER NEED

_____

_____

_____

Scripture

_____

_____

_____

Date Prayer Answered/Confirmed

_____

_____

_____

PRAYER NEED

_____

_____

_____

Scripture

_____

_____

_____

Date Prayer Answered/Confirmed

_____

_____

_____

PRAYER NEED

_____
_____
_____

Scripture

_____
_____
_____

Date Prayer Answered/Confirmed

_____
_____
_____

PRAYER NEED

_____
_____
_____

Scripture

_____
_____
_____

Date Prayer Answered/Confirmed

_____
_____
_____

Ruby W. Smith, B.S., M.S., N.D.

PRAYER NEED

_____

_____

_____

Scripture

_____

_____

_____

Date Prayer Answered/Confirmed

_____

_____

_____

PRAYER NEED

_____

_____

_____

Scripture

_____

_____

_____

Date Prayer Answered/Confirmed

_____

_____

_____

PRAYER NEED

_____

_____

_____

Scripture

_____

_____

_____

Date Prayer Answered/Confirmed

_____

_____

_____

PRAYER NEED

_____

_____

_____

Scripture

_____

_____

_____

Date Prayer Answered/Confirmed

_____

_____

_____

PRAYER NEED

_____

_____

_____

Scripture

_____

_____

_____

Date Prayer Answered/Confirmed

_____

_____

_____

PRAYER NEED

_____

_____

_____

Scripture

_____

_____

_____

Date Prayer Answered/Confirmed

_____

_____

_____

PRAYER NEED

_____

_____

_____

Scripture

_____

_____

_____

Date Prayer Answered/Confirmed

_____

_____

_____

PRAYER NEED

_____

_____

_____

Scripture

_____

_____

_____

Date Prayer Answered/Confirmed

_____

_____

_____

PRAYER NEED

_____

_____

_____

Scripture

_____

_____

_____

Date Prayer Answered/Confirmed

_____

_____

_____

PRAYER NEED

_____

_____

_____

Scripture

_____

_____

_____

Date Prayer Answered/Confirmed

_____

_____

_____

PRAYER NEED

_____

_____

_____

Scripture

_____

_____

_____

Date Prayer Answered/Confirmed

_____

_____

_____

PRAYER NEED

_____

_____

_____

Scripture

_____

_____

_____

Date Prayer Answered/Confirmed

_____

_____

_____

PRAYER NEED

_____

_____

_____

Scripture

_____

_____

_____

Date Prayer Answered/Confirmed

_____

_____

_____

PRAYER NEED

_____

_____

_____

Scripture

_____

_____

_____

Date Prayer Answered/Confirmed

_____

_____

_____

PRAYER NEED

_____
_____
_____

Scripture

_____
_____
_____

Date Prayer Answered/Confirmed

_____
_____
_____

PRAYER NEED

_____
_____
_____

Scripture

_____
_____
_____

Date Prayer Answered/Confirmed

_____
_____
_____

PRAYER NEED

_____

_____

_____

Scripture

_____

_____

_____

Date Prayer Answered/Confirmed

_____

_____

_____

PRAYER NEED

_____

_____

_____

Scripture

_____

_____

_____

Date Prayer Answered/Confirmed

_____

_____

_____

PRAYER NEED

_____

_____

_____

Scripture

_____

_____

_____

Date Prayer Answered/Confirmed

_____

_____

_____

PRAYER NEED

_____

_____

_____

Scripture

_____

_____

_____

Date Prayer Answered/Confirmed

_____

_____

_____

PRAYER NEED

_____

_____

_____

Scripture

_____

_____

_____

Date Prayer Answered/Confirmed

_____

_____

_____

PRAYER NEED

_____

_____

_____

Scripture

_____

_____

_____

Date Prayer Answered/Confirmed

_____

_____

_____

PRAYER NEED

_____

_____

_____

Scripture

_____

_____

_____

Date Prayer Answered/Confirmed

_____

_____

_____

PRAYER NEED

_____

_____

_____

Scripture

_____

_____

_____

Date Prayer Answered/Confirmed

_____

_____

_____

PRAYER NEED

_____

_____

_____

Scripture

_____

_____

_____

Date Prayer Answered/Confirmed

_____

_____

_____

PRAYER NEED

_____

_____

_____

Scripture

_____

_____

_____

Date Prayer Answered/Confirmed

_____

_____

_____

PRAYER NEED

_____

_____

_____

Scripture

_____

_____

_____

Date Prayer Answered/Confirmed

_____

_____

_____

PRAYER NEED

_____

_____

_____

Scripture

_____

_____

_____

Date Prayer Answered/Confirmed

_____

_____

_____

PRAYER NEED

_____

_____

_____

Scripture

_____

_____

_____

Date Prayer Answered/Confirmed

_____

_____

_____

PRAYER NEED

_____

_____

_____

Scripture

_____

_____

_____

Date Prayer Answered/Confirmed

_____

_____

_____

PRAYER NEED

_____

_____

_____

Scripture

_____

_____

_____

Date Prayer Answered/Confirmed

_____

_____

_____

PRAYER NEED

_____

_____

_____

Scripture

_____

_____

_____

Date Prayer Answered/Confirmed

_____

_____

_____

PRAYER NEED

_____

_____

_____

Scripture

_____

_____

_____

Date Prayer Answered/Confirmed

_____

_____

_____

PRAYER NEED

_____

_____

_____

Scripture

_____

_____

_____

Date Prayer Answered/Confirmed

_____

_____

_____

PRAYER NEED

_____
_____
_____

Scripture

_____
_____
_____

Date Prayer Answered/Confirmed

_____
_____
_____

PRAYER NEED

_____
_____
_____

Scripture

_____
_____
_____

Date Prayer Answered/Confirmed

_____
_____
_____

PRAYER NEED

_____

_____

_____

Scripture

_____

_____

_____

Date Prayer Answered/Confirmed

_____

_____

_____

PRAYER NEED

_____

_____

_____

Scripture

_____

_____

_____

Date Prayer Answered/Confirmed

_____

_____

_____

PRAYER NEED

_____

_____

_____

Scripture

_____

_____

_____

Date Prayer Answered/Confirmed

_____

_____

_____

PRAYER NEED

_____

_____

_____

Scripture

_____

_____

_____

Date Prayer Answered/Confirmed

_____

_____

_____

PRAYER NEED

_____

_____

_____

Scripture

_____

_____

_____

Date Prayer Answered/Confirmed

_____

_____

_____

PRAYER NEED

_____

_____

_____

Scripture

_____

_____

_____

Date Prayer Answered/Confirmed

_____

_____

_____

PRAYER NEED

_____

_____

_____

Scripture

_____

_____

_____

Date Prayer Answered/Confirmed

_____

_____

_____

PRAYER NEED

_____

_____

_____

Scripture

_____

_____

_____

Date Prayer Answered/Confirmed

_____

_____

_____

PRAYER NEED

_____

_____

_____

Scripture

_____

_____

_____

Date Prayer Answered/Confirmed

_____

_____

_____

PRAYER NEED

_____

_____

_____

Scripture

_____

_____

_____

Date Prayer Answered/Confirmed

_____

_____

_____

PRAYER NEED

_____

_____

_____

Scripture

_____

_____

_____

Date Prayer Answered/Confirmed

_____

_____

_____

PRAYER NEED

_____

_____

_____

Scripture

_____

_____

_____

Date Prayer Answered/Confirmed

_____

_____

_____

PRAYER NEED

_____

_____

_____

Scripture

_____

_____

_____

Date Prayer Answered/Confirmed

_____

_____

_____

PRAYER NEED

_____

_____

_____

Scripture

_____

_____

_____

Date Prayer Answered/Confirmed

_____

_____

_____

PRAYER NEED

_____

_____

_____

Scripture

_____

_____

_____

Date Prayer Answered/Confirmed

_____

_____

_____

PRAYER NEED

_____

_____

_____

Scripture

_____

_____

_____

Date Prayer Answered/Confirmed

_____

_____

_____

PRAYER NEED

_____

_____

_____

Scripture

_____

_____

_____

Date Prayer Answered/Confirmed

_____

_____

_____

PRAYER NEED

_____

_____

_____

Scripture

_____

_____

_____

Date Prayer Answered/Confirmed

_____

_____

_____

PRAYER NEED

_____

_____

_____

Scripture

_____

_____

_____

Date Prayer Answered/Confirmed

_____

_____

_____

PRAYER NEED

_____

_____

_____

Scripture

_____

_____

_____

Date Prayer Answered/Confirmed

_____

_____

_____

PRAYER NEED

_____

_____

_____

Scripture

_____

_____

_____

Date Prayer Answered/Confirmed

_____

_____

_____

PRAYER NEED

_____

_____

_____

Scripture

_____

_____

_____

Date Prayer Answered/Confirmed

_____

_____

_____

PRAYER NEED

_____

_____

_____

Scripture

_____

_____

_____

Date Prayer Answered/Confirmed

_____

_____

_____

PRAYER NEED

_____

_____

_____

Scripture

_____

_____

_____

Date Prayer Answered/Confirmed

_____

_____

_____

PRAYER NEED

_____

_____

_____

Scripture

_____

_____

_____

Date Prayer Answered/Confirmed

_____

_____

_____

PRAYER NEED

_____

_____

_____

Scripture

_____

_____

_____

Date Prayer Answered/Confirmed

_____

_____

_____

PRAYER NEED

_____

_____

_____

Scripture

_____

_____

_____

Date Prayer Answered/Confirmed

_____

_____

_____

PRAYER NEED

_____

_____

_____

Scripture

_____

_____

_____

Date Prayer Answered/Confirmed

_____

_____

_____

PRAYER NEED

_____

_____

_____

Scripture

_____

_____

_____

Date Prayer Answered/Confirmed

_____

_____

_____

PRAYER NEED

_____

_____

_____

Scripture

_____

_____

_____

Date Prayer Answered/Confirmed

_____

_____

_____

PRAYER NEED

_____

_____

_____

Scripture

_____

_____

_____

Date Prayer Answered/Confirmed

_____

_____

_____

PRAYER NEED

_____

_____

_____

Scripture

_____

_____

_____

Date Prayer Answered/Confirmed

_____

_____

_____

Ruby W. Smith, B.S., M.S., N.D.

PRAYER NEED

_____

_____

_____

Scripture

_____

_____

_____

Date Prayer Answered/Confirmed

_____

_____

_____

PRAYER NEED

_____

_____

_____

Scripture

_____

_____

_____

Date Prayer Answered/Confirmed

_____

_____

_____

PRAYER NEED

_____

_____

_____

Scripture

_____

_____

_____

Date Prayer Answered/Confirmed

_____

_____

_____

PRAYER NEED

_____

_____

_____

Scripture

_____

_____

_____

Date Prayer Answered/Confirmed

_____

_____

_____

PRAYER NEED

_____

_____

_____

Scripture

_____

_____

_____

Date Prayer Answered/Confirmed

_____

_____

_____

PRAYER NEED

_____

_____

_____

Scripture

_____

_____

_____

Date Prayer Answered/Confirmed

_____

_____

_____

PRAYER NEED

_____

_____

_____

Scripture

_____

_____

_____

Date Prayer Answered/Confirmed

_____

_____

_____

PRAYER NEED

_____

_____

_____

Scripture

_____

_____

_____

Date Prayer Answered/Confirmed

_____

_____

_____

Ruby W. Smith, B.S., M.S., N.D.

PRAYER NEED

_____

_____

_____

Scripture

_____

_____

_____

Date Prayer Answered/Confirmed

_____

_____

_____

PRAYER NEED

_____

_____

_____

Scripture

_____

_____

_____

Date Prayer Answered/Confirmed

_____

_____

_____

PRAYER NEED

_____
_____
_____

Scripture

_____
_____
_____

Date Prayer Answered/Confirmed

_____
_____
_____

PRAYER NEED

_____
_____
_____

Scripture

_____
_____
_____

Date Prayer Answered/Confirmed

_____
_____
_____

PRAYER NEED

_____

_____

_____

Scripture

_____

_____

_____

Date Prayer Answered/Confirmed

_____

_____

_____

PRAYER NEED

_____

_____

_____

Scripture

_____

_____

_____

Date Prayer Answered/Confirmed

_____

_____

_____

PRAYER NEED

_____

_____

_____

Scripture

_____

_____

_____

Date Prayer Answered/Confirmed

_____

_____

_____

PRAYER NEED

_____

_____

_____

Scripture

_____

_____

_____

Date Prayer Answered/Confirmed

_____

_____

_____

PRAYER NEED

_____

_____

_____

Scripture

_____

_____

_____

Date Prayer Answered/Confirmed

_____

_____

_____

PRAYER NEED

_____

_____

_____

Scripture

_____

_____

Date Prayer Answered/Confirmed

_____

_____

_____

PRAYER NEED

_____

_____

_____

Scripture

_____

_____

_____

Date Prayer Answered/Confirmed

_____

_____

_____

PRAYER NEED

_____

_____

_____

Scripture

_____

_____

_____

Date Prayer Answered/Confirmed

_____

_____

_____

Ruby W. Smith, B.S., M.S., N.D.

PRAYER NEED

_____

_____

_____

Scripture

_____

_____

_____

Date Prayer Answered/Confirmed

_____

_____

_____

PRAYER NEED

_____

_____

_____

Scripture

_____

_____

_____

Date Prayer Answered/Confirmed

_____

_____

_____

PRAYER NEED

_____

_____

_____

Scripture

_____

_____

_____

Date Prayer Answered/Confirmed

_____

_____

_____

PRAYER NEED

_____

_____

_____

Scripture

_____

_____

_____

Date Prayer Answered/Confirmed

_____

_____

_____

PRAYER NEED

_____

_____

_____

Scripture

_____

_____

_____

Date Prayer Answered/Confirmed

_____

_____

_____

PRAYER NEED

_____

_____

_____

Scripture

_____

_____

_____

Date Prayer Answered/Confirmed

_____

_____

_____

PRAYER NEED

_____

_____

_____

Scripture

_____

_____

_____

Date Prayer Answered/Confirmed

_____

_____

_____

PRAYER NEED

_____

_____

_____

Scripture

_____

_____

_____

Date Prayer Answered/Confirmed

_____

_____

_____

PRAYER NEED

_____

_____

_____

Scripture

_____

_____

_____

Date Prayer Answered/Confirmed

_____

_____

_____

PRAYER NEED

_____

_____

_____

Scripture

_____

_____

_____

Date Prayer Answered/Confirmed

_____

_____

_____

PRAYER NEED

_____

_____

_____

Scripture

_____

_____

_____

Date Prayer Answered/Confirmed

_____

_____

_____

PRAYER NEED

_____

_____

_____

Scripture

_____

_____

_____

Date Prayer Answered/Confirmed

_____

_____

_____

PRAYER NEED

_____

_____

_____

Scripture

_____

_____

_____

Date Prayer Answered/Confirmed

_____

_____

_____

PRAYER NEED

_____

_____

_____

Scripture

_____

_____

_____

Date Prayer Answered/Confirmed

_____

_____

_____

PRAYER NEED

_____

_____

_____

Scripture

_____

_____

_____

Date Prayer Answered/Confirmed

_____

_____

_____

PRAYER NEED

_____

_____

_____

Scripture

_____

_____

_____

Date Prayer Answered/Confirmed

_____

_____

_____

PRAYER NEED

_____

_____

_____

Scripture

_____

_____

_____

Date Prayer Answered/Confirmed

_____

_____

_____

PRAYER NEED

_____

_____

_____

Scripture

_____

_____

_____

Date Prayer Answered/Confirmed

_____

_____

_____

PRAYER NEED

_____

_____

_____

Scripture

_____

_____

_____

Date Prayer Answered/Confirmed

_____

_____

_____

PRAYER NEED

_____

_____

_____

Scripture

_____

_____

_____

Date Prayer Answered/Confirmed

_____

_____

_____

PRAYER NEED

_____

_____

_____

Scripture

_____

_____

_____

Date Prayer Answered/Confirmed

_____

_____

_____

PRAYER NEED

_____

_____

_____

Scripture

_____

_____

_____

Date Prayer Answered/Confirmed

_____

_____

_____

PRAYER NEED

_____

_____

_____

Scripture

_____

_____

_____

Date Prayer Answered/Confirmed

_____

_____

_____

PRAYER NEED

_____

_____

_____

Scripture

_____

_____

_____

Date Prayer Answered/Confirmed

_____

_____

_____

PRAYER NEED

_____

_____

_____

Scripture

_____

_____

_____

Date Prayer Answered/Confirmed

_____

_____

_____

PRAYER NEED

_____

_____

_____

Scripture

_____

_____

_____

Date Prayer Answered/Confirmed

_____

_____

_____

PRAYER NEED

_____

_____

_____

Scripture

_____

_____

_____

Date Prayer Answered/Confirmed

_____

_____

_____

PRAYER NEED

_____

_____

_____

Scripture

_____

_____

_____

Date Prayer Answered/Confirmed

_____

_____

_____

PRAYER NEED

_____

_____

_____

Scripture

_____

_____

_____

Date Prayer Answered/Confirmed

_____

_____

_____

PRAYER NEED

_____

_____

_____

Scripture

_____

_____

_____

Date Prayer Answered/Confirmed

_____

_____

_____

PRAYER NEED

_____

_____

_____

Scripture

_____

_____

_____

Date Prayer Answered/Confirmed

_____

_____

_____

PRAYER NEED

_____

_____

_____

Scripture

_____

_____

_____

Date Prayer Answered/Confirmed

_____

_____

_____

Ruby W. Smith, B.S., M.S., N.D.

PRAYER NEED

_____

_____

_____

Scripture

_____

_____

_____

Date Prayer Answered/Confirmed

_____

_____

_____

PRAYER NEED

_____

_____

_____

Scripture

_____

_____

_____

Date Prayer Answered/Confirmed

_____

_____

_____

PRAYER NEED

_____

_____

_____

Scripture

_____

_____

_____

Date Prayer Answered/Confirmed

_____

_____

_____

PRAYER NEED

_____

_____

_____

Scripture

_____

_____

_____

Date Prayer Answered/Confirmed

_____

_____

_____

PRAYER NEED

_____

_____

_____

Scripture

_____

_____

_____

Date Prayer Answered/Confirmed

_____

_____

_____

PRAYER NEED

_____

_____

_____

Scripture

_____

_____

_____

Date Prayer Answered/Confirmed

_____

_____

_____

PRAYER NEED

_____

_____

_____

Scripture

_____

_____

_____

Date Prayer Answered/Confirmed

_____

_____

_____

PRAYER NEED

_____

_____

_____

Scripture

_____

_____

_____

Date Prayer Answered/Confirmed

_____

_____

_____

Ruby W. Smith, B.S., M.S., N.D.

PRAYER NEED

_____

_____

_____

Scripture

_____

_____

_____

Date Prayer Answered/Confirmed

_____

_____

_____

PRAYER NEED

_____

_____

_____

Scripture

_____

_____

_____

Date Prayer Answered/Confirmed

_____

_____

_____

PRAYER NEED

_____

_____

_____

Scripture

_____

_____

_____

Date Prayer Answered/Confirmed

_____

_____

_____

PRAYER NEED

_____

_____

_____

Scripture

_____

_____

_____

Date Prayer Answered/Confirmed

_____

_____

_____

PRAYER NEED

_____

_____

_____

Scripture

_____

_____

_____

Date Prayer Answered/Confirmed

_____

_____

_____

PRAYER NEED

_____

_____

_____

Scripture

_____

_____

_____

Date Prayer Answered/Confirmed

_____

_____

_____

PRAYER NEED

_____

_____

_____

Scripture

_____

_____

_____

Date Prayer Answered/Confirmed

_____

_____

_____

PRAYER NEED

_____

_____

_____

Scripture

_____

_____

_____

Date Prayer Answered/Confirmed

_____

_____

_____

Ruby W. Smith, B.S., M.S., N.D.

PRAYER NEED

_____

_____

_____

Scripture

_____

_____

_____

Date Prayer Answered/Confirmed

_____

_____

_____

PRAYER NEED

_____

_____

_____

Scripture

_____

_____

_____

Date Prayer Answered/Confirmed

_____

_____

_____

PRAYER NEED

_____

_____

_____

Scripture

_____

_____

_____

Date Prayer Answered/Confirmed

_____

_____

_____

PRAYER NEED

_____

_____

_____

Scripture

_____

_____

_____

Date Prayer Answered/Confirmed

_____

_____

_____

PRAYER NEED

_____

_____

_____

Scripture

_____

_____

_____

Date Prayer Answered/Confirmed

_____

_____

_____

PRAYER NEED

_____

_____

_____

Scripture

_____

_____

_____

Date Prayer Answered/Confirmed

_____

_____

_____

PRAYER NEED

_____
_____
_____

Scripture

_____
_____
_____

Date Prayer Answered/Confirmed

_____
_____
_____

PRAYER NEED

_____
_____
_____

Scripture

_____
_____
_____

Date Prayer Answered/Confirmed

_____
_____
_____

PRAYER NEED

_____

_____

_____

Scripture

_____

_____

_____

Date Prayer Answered/Confirmed

_____

_____

_____

PRAYER NEED

_____

_____

_____

Scripture

_____

_____

_____

Date Prayer Answered/Confirmed

_____

_____

_____

PRAYER NEED

_____

_____

_____

Scripture

_____

_____

_____

Date Prayer Answered/Confirmed

_____

_____

_____

PRAYER NEED

_____

_____

_____

Scripture

_____

_____

_____

Date Prayer Answered/Confirmed

_____

_____

_____

PRAYER NEED

_____

_____

_____

Scripture

_____

_____

_____

Date Prayer Answered/Confirmed

_____

_____

_____

PRAYER NEED

_____

_____

_____

Scripture

_____

_____

_____

Date Prayer Answered/Confirmed

_____

_____

_____

PRAYER NEED

_____
_____
_____

Scripture

_____
_____
_____

Date Prayer Answered/Confirmed

_____
_____
_____

PRAYER NEED

_____
_____
_____

Scripture

_____
_____
_____

Date Prayer Answered/Confirmed

_____
_____
_____

PRAYER NEED

_____

_____

_____

Scripture

_____

_____

_____

Date Prayer Answered/Confirmed

_____

_____

_____

PRAYER NEED

_____

_____

_____

Scripture

_____

_____

_____

Date Prayer Answered/Confirmed

_____

_____

_____

PRAYER NEED

_____
_____
_____

Scripture

_____
_____
_____

Date Prayer Answered/Confirmed

_____
_____
_____

PRAYER NEED

_____
_____
_____

Scripture

_____
_____
_____

Date Prayer Answered/Confirmed

_____
_____
_____

Ruby W. Smith, B.S., M.S., N.D.

PRAYER NEED

_____

_____

_____

Scripture

_____

_____

_____

Date Prayer Answered/Confirmed

_____

_____

_____

PRAYER NEED

_____

_____

_____

Scripture

_____

_____

_____

Date Prayer Answered/Confirmed

_____

_____

_____

PRAYER NEED

_____

_____

_____

Scripture

_____

_____

_____

Date Prayer Answered/Confirmed

_____

_____

_____

PRAYER NEED

_____

_____

_____

Scripture

_____

_____

_____

Date Prayer Answered/Confirmed

_____

_____

_____

Ruby W. Smith, B.S., M.S., N.D.

PRAYER NEED

_____

_____

_____

Scripture

_____

_____

_____

Date Prayer Answered/Confirmed

_____

_____

_____

PRAYER NEED

_____

_____

_____

Scripture

_____

_____

_____

Date Prayer Answered/Confirmed

_____

_____

_____

PRAYER NEED

_____

_____

_____

Scripture

_____

_____

_____

Date Prayer Answered/Confirmed

_____

_____

_____

PRAYER NEED

_____

_____

_____

Scripture

_____

_____

_____

Date Prayer Answered/Confirmed

_____

_____

_____

PRAYER NEED

_____

_____

_____

Scripture

_____

_____

_____

Date Prayer Answered/Confirmed

_____

_____

_____

PRAYER NEED

_____

_____

_____

Scripture

_____

_____

_____

Date Prayer Answered/Confirmed

_____

_____

_____

PRAYER NEED

_____

_____

_____

Scripture

_____

_____

_____

Date Prayer Answered/Confirmed

_____

_____

_____

PRAYER NEED

_____

_____

_____

Scripture

_____

_____

_____

Date Prayer Answered/Confirmed

_____

_____

_____

PRAYER NEED

_____

_____

_____

Scripture

_____

_____

_____

Date Prayer Answered/Confirmed

_____

_____

_____

PRAYER NEED

_____

_____

_____

Scripture

_____

_____

_____

Date Prayer Answered/Confirmed

_____

_____

_____

PRAYER NEED

_____
_____
_____

Scripture

_____
_____
_____

Date Prayer Answered/Confirmed

_____
_____
_____

PRAYER NEED

_____
_____
_____

Scripture

_____
_____
_____

Date Prayer Answered/Confirmed

_____
_____
_____

PRAYER NEED

_____

_____

_____

Scripture

_____

_____

_____

Date Prayer Answered/Confirmed

_____

_____

_____

PRAYER NEED

_____

_____

_____

Scripture

_____

_____

_____

Date Prayer Answered/Confirmed

_____

_____

_____

PRAYER NEED

_____

_____

_____

Scripture

_____

_____

_____

Date Prayer Answered/Confirmed

_____

_____

_____

PRAYER NEED

_____

_____

_____

Scripture

_____

_____

_____

Date Prayer Answered/Confirmed

_____

_____

_____

PRAYER NEED

_____

_____

_____

Scripture

_____

_____

_____

Date Prayer Answered/Confirmed

_____

_____

_____

PRAYER NEED

_____

_____

_____

Scripture

_____

_____

_____

Date Prayer Answered/Confirmed

_____

_____

_____

PRAYER NEED

_____

_____

_____

Scripture

_____

_____

_____

Date Prayer Answered/Confirmed

_____

_____

_____

PRAYER NEED

_____

_____

_____

Scripture

_____

_____

_____

Date Prayer Answered/Confirmed

_____

_____

_____

PRAYER NEED

_____

_____

_____

Scripture

_____

_____

_____

Date Prayer Answered/Confirmed

_____

_____

_____

PRAYER NEED

_____

_____

_____

Scripture

_____

_____

_____

Date Prayer Answered/Confirmed

_____

_____

_____

PRAYER NEED

_____

_____

_____

Scripture

_____

_____

_____

Date Prayer Answered/Confirmed

_____

_____

_____

PRAYER NEED

_____

_____

_____

Scripture

_____

_____

_____

Date Prayer Answered/Confirmed

_____

_____

_____

PRAYER NEED

_____

_____

_____

Scripture

_____

_____

_____

Date Prayer Answered/Confirmed

_____

_____

_____

PRAYER NEED

_____

_____

_____

Scripture

_____

_____

_____

Date Prayer Answered/Confirmed

_____

_____

_____

PRAYER NEED

_____

_____

_____

Scripture

_____

_____

_____

Date Prayer Answered/Confirmed

_____

_____

_____

PRAYER NEED

_____

_____

_____

Scripture

_____

_____

_____

Date Prayer Answered/Confirmed

_____

_____

_____

PRAYER NEED

_____

_____

_____

Scripture

_____

_____

_____

Date Prayer Answered/Confirmed

_____

_____

_____

PRAYER NEED

_____

_____

_____

Scripture

_____

_____

_____

Date Prayer Answered/Confirmed

_____

_____

_____

PRAYER NEED

_____

_____

_____

Scripture

_____

_____

_____

Date Prayer Answered/Confirmed

_____

_____

_____

PRAYER NEED

_____

_____

_____

Scripture

_____

_____

_____

Date Prayer Answered/Confirmed

_____

_____

_____

Ruby W. Smith, B.S., M.S., N.D.

PRAYER NEED

_____

_____

_____

Scripture

_____

_____

_____

Date Prayer Answered/Confirmed

_____

_____

_____

PRAYER NEED

_____

_____

_____

Scripture

_____

_____

_____

Date Prayer Answered/Confirmed

_____

_____

_____

PRAYER NEED

_____

_____

_____

Scripture

_____

_____

_____

Date Prayer Answered/Confirmed

_____

_____

_____

PRAYER NEED

_____

_____

_____

Scripture

_____

_____

_____

Date Prayer Answered/Confirmed

_____

_____

_____

PRAYER NEED

_____

_____

_____

Scripture

_____

_____

_____

Date Prayer Answered/Confirmed

_____

_____

_____

PRAYER NEED

_____

_____

_____

Scripture

_____

_____

_____

Date Prayer Answered/Confirmed

_____

_____

_____

PRAYER NEED

_____

_____

_____

Scripture

_____

_____

_____

Date Prayer Answered/Confirmed

_____

_____

_____

PRAYER NEED

_____

_____

_____

Scripture

_____

_____

_____

Date Prayer Answered/Confirmed

_____

_____

_____

PRAYER NEED

_____

_____

_____

Scripture

_____

_____

_____

Date Prayer Answered/Confirmed

_____

_____

_____

PRAYER NEED

_____

_____

_____

Scripture

_____

_____

_____

Date Prayer Answered/Confirmed

_____

_____

_____

PRAYER NEED

_____

_____

_____

Scripture

_____

_____

_____

Date Prayer Answered/Confirmed

_____

_____

_____

PRAYER NEED

_____

_____

_____

Scripture

_____

_____

_____

Date Prayer Answered/Confirmed

_____

_____

_____

PRAYER NEED

_____

_____

_____

Scripture

_____

_____

_____

Date Prayer Answered/Confirmed

_____

_____

_____

PRAYER NEED

_____

_____

_____

Scripture

_____

_____

_____

Date Prayer Answered/Confirmed

_____

_____

_____

PRAYER NEED

_____

_____

_____

Scripture

_____

_____

_____

Date Prayer Answered/Confirmed

_____

_____

_____

PRAYER NEED

_____

_____

_____

Scripture

_____

_____

_____

Date Prayer Answered/Confirmed

_____

_____

_____

PRAYER NEED

_____

_____

_____

Scripture

_____

_____

_____

Date Prayer Answered/Confirmed

_____

_____

_____

PRAYER NEED

_____

_____

_____

Scripture

_____

_____

_____

Date Prayer Answered/Confirmed

_____

_____

_____

PRAYER NEED

_____
_____
_____

Scripture

_____
_____
_____

Date Prayer Answered/Confirmed

_____
_____
_____

PRAYER NEED

_____
_____
_____

Scripture

_____
_____
_____

Date Prayer Answered/Confirmed

_____
_____
_____

Ruby W. Smith, B.S., M.S., N.D.

PRAYER NEED

_____

_____

_____

Scripture

_____

_____

_____

Date Prayer Answered/Confirmed

_____

_____

_____

PRAYER NEED

_____

_____

_____

Scripture

_____

_____

_____

Date Prayer Answered/Confirmed

_____

_____

_____

PRAYER NEED

_____

_____

_____

Scripture

_____

_____

_____

Date Prayer Answered/Confirmed

_____

_____

_____

PRAYER NEED

_____

_____

_____

Scripture

_____

_____

_____

Date Prayer Answered/Confirmed

_____

_____

_____

Ruby W. Smith, B.S., M.S., N.D.

PRAYER NEED

_____

_____

_____

Scripture

_____

_____

_____

Date Prayer Answered/Confirmed

_____

_____

_____

PRAYER NEED

_____

_____

_____

Scripture

_____

_____

_____

Date Prayer Answered/Confirmed

_____

_____

_____

PRAYER NEED

_____

_____

_____

Scripture

_____

_____

_____

Date Prayer Answered/Confirmed

_____

_____

_____

PRAYER NEED

_____

_____

_____

Scripture

_____

_____

_____

Date Prayer Answered/Confirmed

_____

_____

_____

Ruby W. Smith, B.S., M.S., N.D.

PRAYER NEED

_____

_____

_____

Scripture

_____

_____

_____

Date Prayer Answered/Confirmed

_____

_____

_____

PRAYER NEED

_____

_____

_____

Scripture

_____

_____

_____

Date Prayer Answered/Confirmed

_____

_____

_____

PRAYER NEED

_____

_____

_____

Scripture

_____

_____

_____

Date Prayer Answered/Confirmed

_____

_____

_____

PRAYER NEED

_____

_____

_____

Scripture

_____

_____

_____

Date Prayer Answered/Confirmed

_____

_____

_____

PRAYER NEED

_____

_____

_____

Scripture

_____

_____

_____

Date Prayer Answered/Confirmed

_____

_____

_____

PRAYER NEED

_____

_____

_____

Scripture

_____

_____

_____

Date Prayer Answered/Confirmed

_____

_____

_____

PRAYER NEED

_____

_____

_____

Scripture

_____

_____

_____

Date Prayer Answered/Confirmed

_____

_____

_____

PRAYER NEED

_____

_____

_____

Scripture

_____

_____

_____

Date Prayer Answered/Confirmed

_____

_____

_____

PRAYER NEED

_____

_____

_____

Scripture

_____

_____

_____

Date Prayer Answered/Confirmed

_____

_____

_____

PRAYER NEED

_____

_____

_____

Scripture

_____

_____

_____

Date Prayer Answered/Confirmed

_____

_____

_____

PRAYER NEED

_____

_____

_____

Scripture

_____

_____

_____

Date Prayer Answered/Confirmed

_____

_____

_____

PRAYER NEED

_____

_____

_____

Scripture

_____

_____

_____

Date Prayer Answered/Confirmed

_____

_____

_____

PRAYER NEED

_____

_____

_____

Scripture

_____

_____

_____

Date Prayer Answered/Confirmed

_____

_____

_____

PRAYER NEED

_____

_____

_____

Scripture

_____

_____

_____

Date Prayer Answered/Confirmed

_____

_____

_____

PRAYER NEED

_____

_____

_____

Scripture

_____

_____

_____

Date Prayer Answered/Confirmed

_____

_____

_____

PRAYER NEED

_____

_____

_____

Scripture

_____

_____

_____

Date Prayer Answered/Confirmed

_____

_____

_____

Ruby W. Smith, B.S., M.S., N.D.

PRAYER NEED

_____

_____

_____

Scripture

_____

_____

_____

Date Prayer Answered/Confirmed

_____

_____

_____

PRAYER NEED

_____

_____

_____

Scripture

_____

_____

_____

Date Prayer Answered/Confirmed

_____

_____

_____

PRAYER NEED

_____

_____

_____

Scripture

_____

_____

_____

Date Prayer Answered/Confirmed

_____

_____

_____

PRAYER NEED

_____

_____

_____

Scripture

_____

_____

_____

Date Prayer Answered/Confirmed

_____

_____

_____

PRAYER NEED

_____

_____

_____

Scripture

_____

_____

_____

Date Prayer Answered/Confirmed

_____

_____

_____

PRAYER NEED

_____

_____

_____

Scripture

_____

_____

_____

Date Prayer Answered/Confirmed

_____

_____

_____

PRAYER NEED

_____

_____

_____

Scripture

_____

_____

_____

Date Prayer Answered/Confirmed

_____

_____

_____

PRAYER NEED

_____

_____

_____

Scripture

_____

_____

_____

Date Prayer Answered/Confirmed

_____

_____

_____

PRAYER NEED

_____

_____

_____

Scripture

_____

_____

_____

Date Prayer Answered/Confirmed

_____

_____

_____

PRAYER NEED

_____

_____

_____

Scripture

_____

_____

_____

Date Prayer Answered/Confirmed

_____

_____

_____

PRAYER NEED

_____

_____

_____

Scripture

_____

_____

_____

Date Prayer Answered/Confirmed

_____

_____

_____

PRAYER NEED

_____

_____

_____

Scripture

_____

_____

_____

Date Prayer Answered/Confirmed

_____

_____

_____

PRAYER NEED

_____

_____

_____

Scripture

_____

_____

_____

Date Prayer Answered/Confirmed

_____

_____

_____

PRAYER NEED

_____

_____

_____

Scripture

_____

_____

_____

Date Prayer Answered/Confirmed

_____

_____

_____

PRAYER NEED

_____

_____

_____

Scripture

_____

_____

_____

Date Prayer Answered/Confirmed

_____

_____

_____

PRAYER NEED

_____

_____

_____

Scripture

_____

_____

_____

Date Prayer Answered/Confirmed

_____

_____

_____

PRAYER NEED

_____

_____

_____

Scripture

_____

_____

_____

Date Prayer Answered/Confirmed

_____

_____

_____

PRAYER NEED

_____

_____

_____

Scripture

_____

_____

_____

Date Prayer Answered/Confirmed

_____

_____

_____

PRAYER NEED

_____

_____

_____

Scripture

_____

_____

_____

Date Prayer Answered/Confirmed

_____

_____

_____

PRAYER NEED

_____

_____

_____

Scripture

_____

_____

_____

Date Prayer Answered/Confirmed

_____

_____

_____

Ruby W. Smith, B.S., M.S., N.D.

PRAYER NEED

_____

_____

_____

Scripture

_____

_____

_____

Date Prayer Answered/Confirmed

_____

_____

_____

PRAYER NEED

_____

_____

_____

Scripture

_____

_____

_____

Date Prayer Answered/Confirmed

_____

_____

_____

PRAYER NEED

_____
_____
_____

Scripture

_____
_____
_____

Date Prayer Answered/Confirmed

_____
_____
_____

PRAYER NEED

_____
_____
_____

Scripture

_____
_____
_____

Date Prayer Answered/Confirmed

_____
_____
_____

Ruby W. Smith, B.S., M.S., N.D.

PRAYER NEED

_____

_____

_____

Scripture

_____

_____

_____

Date Prayer Answered/Confirmed

_____

_____

_____

PRAYER NEED

_____

_____

_____

Scripture

_____

_____

_____

Date Prayer Answered/Confirmed

_____

_____

_____

PRAYER NEED

_____

_____

_____

Scripture

_____

_____

_____

Date Prayer Answered/Confirmed

_____

_____

_____

PRAYER NEED

_____

_____

_____

Scripture

_____

_____

_____

Date Prayer Answered/Confirmed

_____

_____

_____

PRAYER NEED

_____

_____

_____

Scripture

_____

_____

_____

Date Prayer Answered/Confirmed

_____

_____

_____

PRAYER NEED

_____

_____

_____

Scripture

_____

_____

_____

Date Prayer Answered/Confirmed

_____

_____

_____

PRAYER NEED

_____

_____

_____

Scripture

_____

_____

_____

Date Prayer Answered/Confirmed

_____

_____

_____

PRAYER NEED

_____

_____

_____

Scripture

_____

_____

_____

Date Prayer Answered/Confirmed

_____

_____

_____

Ruby W. Smith, B.S., M.S., N.D.

PRAYER NEED

_____

_____

_____

Scripture

_____

_____

_____

Date Prayer Answered/Confirmed

_____

_____

_____

PRAYER NEED

_____

_____

_____

Scripture

_____

_____

_____

Date Prayer Answered/Confirmed

_____

_____

_____

PRAYER NEED

_____

_____

_____

Scripture

_____

_____

_____

Date Prayer Answered/Confirmed

_____

_____

_____

PRAYER NEED

_____

_____

_____

Scripture

_____

_____

_____

Date Prayer Answered/Confirmed

_____

_____

_____

Ruby W. Smith, B.S., M.S., N.D.

PRAYER NEED

_____

_____

_____

Scripture

_____

_____

_____

Date Prayer Answered/Confirmed

_____

_____

_____

PRAYER NEED

_____

_____

_____

Scripture

_____

_____

_____

Date Prayer Answered/Confirmed

_____

_____

_____

PRAYER NEED

_____

_____

_____

Scripture

_____

_____

_____

Date Prayer Answered/Confirmed

_____

_____

_____

PRAYER NEED

_____

_____

_____

Scripture

_____

_____

_____

Date Prayer Answered/Confirmed

_____

_____

_____

PRAYER NEED

_____

_____

_____

Scripture

_____

_____

_____

Date Prayer Answered/Confirmed

_____

_____

_____

PRAYER NEED

_____

_____

_____

Scripture

_____

_____

_____

Date Prayer Answered/Confirmed

_____

_____

_____

PRAYER NEED

_____
_____
_____

Scripture

_____
_____
_____

Date Prayer Answered/Confirmed

_____
_____
_____

PRAYER NEED

_____
_____
_____

Scripture

_____
_____
_____

Date Prayer Answered/Confirmed

_____
_____
_____

PRAYER NEED

_____

_____

_____

Scripture

_____

_____

_____

Date Prayer Answered/Confirmed

_____

_____

_____

PRAYER NEED

_____

_____

_____

Scripture

_____

_____

_____

Date Prayer Answered/Confirmed

_____

_____

_____

PRAYER NEED

_____

_____

_____

Scripture

_____

_____

_____

Date Prayer Answered/Confirmed

_____

_____

_____

PRAYER NEED

_____

_____

_____

Scripture

_____

_____

_____

Date Prayer Answered/Confirmed

_____

_____

_____

PRAYER NEED

_____

_____

_____

Scripture

_____

_____

_____

Date Prayer Answered/Confirmed

_____

_____

_____

PRAYER NEED

_____

_____

_____

Scripture

_____

_____

_____

Date Prayer Answered/Confirmed

_____

_____

_____

PRAYER NEED

_____

_____

_____

Scripture

_____

_____

_____

Date Prayer Answered/Confirmed

_____

_____

_____

PRAYER NEED

_____

_____

_____

Scripture

_____

_____

_____

Date Prayer Answered/Confirmed

_____

_____

_____

PRAYER NEED

_____

_____

_____

Scripture

_____

_____

_____

Date Prayer Answered/Confirmed

_____

_____

_____

PRAYER NEED

_____

_____

_____

Scripture

_____

_____

_____

Date Prayer Answered/Confirmed

_____

_____

_____

PRAYER NEED

_____

_____

_____

Scripture

_____

_____

_____

Date Prayer Answered/Confirmed

_____

_____

_____

PRAYER NEED

_____

_____

_____

Scripture

_____

_____

_____

Date Prayer Answered/Confirmed

_____

_____

_____

PRAYER NEED

_____

_____

_____

Scripture

_____

_____

_____

Date Prayer Answered/Confirmed

_____

_____

_____

PRAYER NEED

_____

_____

_____

Scripture

_____

_____

_____

Date Prayer Answered/Confirmed

_____

_____

_____

PRAYER NEED

_____

_____

_____

Scripture

_____

_____

_____

Date Prayer Answered/Confirmed

_____

_____

_____

PRAYER NEED

_____

_____

_____

Scripture

_____

_____

_____

Date Prayer Answered/Confirmed

_____

_____

_____

Ruby W. Smith, B.S., M.S., N.D.

PRAYER NEED

_____

_____

_____

Scripture

_____

_____

_____

Date Prayer Answered/Confirmed

_____

_____

_____

PRAYER NEED

_____

_____

_____

Scripture

_____

_____

_____

Date Prayer Answered/Confirmed

_____

_____

_____

PRAYER NEED

_____

_____

_____

Scripture

_____

_____

_____

Date Prayer Answered/Confirmed

_____

_____

_____

PRAYER NEED

_____

_____

_____

Scripture

_____

_____

_____

Date Prayer Answered/Confirmed

_____

_____

_____

PRAYER NEED

_____

_____

_____

Scripture

_____

_____

_____

Date Prayer Answered/Confirmed

_____

_____

_____

PRAYER NEED

_____

_____

_____

Scripture

_____

_____

_____

Date Prayer Answered/Confirmed

_____

_____

_____

PRAYER NEED

_____
_____
_____

Scripture

_____
_____
_____

Date Prayer Answered/Confirmed

_____
_____
_____

PRAYER NEED

_____
_____
_____

Scripture

_____
_____

Date Prayer Answered/Confirmed

_____
_____
_____

PRAYER NEED

_____

_____

_____

Scripture

_____

_____

_____

Date Prayer Answered/Confirmed

_____

_____

_____

PRAYER NEED

_____

_____

_____

Scripture

_____

_____

_____

Date Prayer Answered/Confirmed

_____

_____

_____

PRAYER NEED

_____

_____

_____

Scripture

_____

_____

_____

Date Prayer Answered/Confirmed

_____

_____

_____

PRAYER NEED

_____

_____

_____

Scripture

_____

_____

_____

Date Prayer Answered/Confirmed

_____

_____

_____

PRAYER NEED

_____

_____

_____

Scripture

_____

_____

_____

Date Prayer Answered/Confirmed

_____

_____

_____

PRAYER NEED

_____

_____

_____

Scripture

_____

_____

_____

Date Prayer Answered/Confirmed

_____

_____

_____

PRAYER NEED

_____
_____
_____

Scripture

_____
_____
_____

Date Prayer Answered/Confirmed

_____
_____
_____

PRAYER NEED

_____
_____
_____

Scripture

_____
_____
_____

Date Prayer Answered/Confirmed

_____
_____
_____

PRAYER NEED

_____

_____

_____

Scripture

_____

_____

_____

Date Prayer Answered/Confirmed

_____

_____

_____

PRAYER NEED

_____

_____

_____

Scripture

_____

_____

_____

Date Prayer Answered/Confirmed

_____

_____

_____

PRAYER NEED

_____
_____
_____

Scripture

_____
_____
_____

Date Prayer Answered/Confirmed

_____
_____
_____

PRAYER NEED

_____
_____
_____

Scripture

_____
_____

Date Prayer Answered/Confirmed

_____
_____
_____

PRAYER NEED

_____

_____

_____

Scripture

_____

_____

_____

Date Prayer Answered/Confirmed

_____

_____

_____

PRAYER NEED

_____

_____

_____

Scripture

_____

_____

_____

Date Prayer Answered/Confirmed

_____

_____

_____

PRAYER NEED

_____

_____

_____

Scripture

_____

_____

_____

Date Prayer Answered/Confirmed

_____

_____

_____

PRAYER NEED

_____

_____

_____

Scripture

_____

_____

_____

Date Prayer Answered/Confirmed

_____

_____

_____

Ruby W. Smith, B.S., M.S., N.D.

PRAYER NEED

_____

_____

_____

Scripture

_____

_____

_____

Date Prayer Answered/Confirmed

_____

_____

_____

PRAYER NEED

_____

_____

_____

Scripture

_____

_____

_____

Date Prayer Answered/Confirmed

_____

_____

_____

PRAYER NEED

_____
_____
_____

Scripture

_____
_____
_____

Date Prayer Answered/Confirmed

_____
_____
_____

PRAYER NEED

_____
_____
_____

Scripture

_____
_____
_____

Date Prayer Answered/Confirmed

_____
_____
_____

PRAYER NEED

_____

_____

_____

Scripture

_____

_____

_____

Date Prayer Answered/Confirmed

_____

_____

_____

PRAYER NEED

_____

_____

_____

Scripture

_____

_____

_____

Date Prayer Answered/Confirmed

_____

_____

_____

PRAYER NEED

_____

_____

_____

Scripture

_____

_____

_____

Date Prayer Answered/Confirmed

_____

_____

_____

PRAYER NEED

_____

_____

_____

Scripture

_____

_____

_____

Date Prayer Answered/Confirmed

_____

_____

_____

PRAYER NEED

_____

_____

_____

Scripture

_____

_____

_____

Date Prayer Answered/Confirmed

_____

_____

_____

PRAYER NEED

_____

_____

_____

Scripture

_____

_____

_____

Date Prayer Answered/Confirmed

_____

_____

_____

PRAYER NEED

_____

_____

_____

Scripture

_____

_____

_____

Date Prayer Answered/Confirmed

_____

_____

_____

PRAYER NEED

_____

_____

_____

Scripture

_____

_____

_____

Date Prayer Answered/Confirmed

_____

_____

_____

PRAYER NEED

_____

_____

_____

Scripture

_____

_____

_____

Date Prayer Answered/Confirmed

_____

_____

_____

PRAYER NEED

_____

_____

_____

Scripture

_____

_____

_____

Date Prayer Answered/Confirmed

_____

_____

_____

PRAYER NEED

_____

_____

_____

Scripture

_____

_____

_____

Date Prayer Answered/Confirmed

_____

_____

_____

PRAYER NEED

_____

_____

_____

Scripture

_____

_____

Date Prayer Answered/Confirmed

_____

_____

_____

Ruby W. Smith, B.S., M.S., N.D.

PRAYER NEED

_____

_____

_____

Scripture

_____

_____

_____

Date Prayer Answered/Confirmed

_____

_____

_____

PRAYER NEED

_____

_____

_____

Scripture

_____

_____

_____

Date Prayer Answered/Confirmed

_____

_____

_____

PRAYER NEED

_____

_____

_____

Scripture

_____

_____

_____

Date Prayer Answered/Confirmed

_____

_____

_____

PRAYER NEED

_____

_____

_____

Scripture

_____

_____

_____

Date Prayer Answered/Confirmed

_____

_____

_____

PRAYER NEED

_____

_____

_____

Scripture

_____

_____

_____

Date Prayer Answered/Confirmed

_____

_____

_____

PRAYER NEED

_____

_____

_____

Scripture

_____

_____

_____

Date Prayer Answered/Confirmed

_____

_____

_____

PRAYER NEED

Scripture

Date Prayer Answered/Confirmed

PRAYER NEED

Scripture

Date Prayer Answered/Confirmed

Ruby W. Smith, B.S., M.S., N.D.

PRAYER NEED

_____

_____

_____

Scripture

_____

_____

_____

Date Prayer Answered/Confirmed

_____

_____

_____

PRAYER NEED

_____

_____

_____

Scripture

_____

_____

_____

Date Prayer Answered/Confirmed

_____

_____

_____

PRAYER NEED

_____

_____

_____

Scripture

_____

_____

_____

Date Prayer Answered/Confirmed

_____

_____

_____

PRAYER NEED

_____

_____

_____

Scripture

_____

_____

_____

Date Prayer Answered/Confirmed

_____

_____

_____

PRAYER NEED

_____

_____

_____

Scripture

_____

_____

_____

Date Prayer Answered/Confirmed

_____

_____

_____

PRAYER NEED

_____

_____

_____

Scripture

_____

_____

_____

Date Prayer Answered/Confirmed

_____

_____

_____

PRAYER NEED

_____

_____

_____

Scripture

_____

_____

_____

Date Prayer Answered/Confirmed

_____

_____

_____

PRAYER NEED

_____

_____

_____

Scripture

_____

_____

_____

Date Prayer Answered/Confirmed

_____

_____

_____

PRAYER NEED

_____

_____

_____

Scripture

_____

_____

_____

Date Prayer Answered/Confirmed

_____

_____

_____

PRAYER NEED

_____

_____

_____

Scripture

_____

_____

_____

Date Prayer Answered/Confirmed

_____

_____

_____

PRAYER NEED

_____

_____

_____

Scripture

_____

_____

_____

Date Prayer Answered/Confirmed

_____

_____

_____

PRAYER NEED

_____

_____

_____

Scripture

_____

_____

_____

Date Prayer Answered/Confirmed

_____

_____

_____

PRAYER NEED

_____

_____

_____

Scripture

_____

_____

_____

Date Prayer Answered/Confirmed

_____

_____

_____

PRAYER NEED

_____

_____

_____

Scripture

_____

_____

_____

Date Prayer Answered/Confirmed

_____

_____

_____

PRAYER NEED

_____

_____

_____

Scripture

_____

_____

_____

Date Prayer Answered/Confirmed

_____

_____

_____

PRAYER NEED

_____

_____

_____

Scripture

_____

_____

_____

Date Prayer Answered/Confirmed

_____

_____

_____

PRAYER NEED

_____

_____

_____

Scripture

_____

_____

_____

Date Prayer Answered/Confirmed

_____

_____

_____

PRAYER NEED

_____

_____

_____

Scripture

_____

_____

_____

Date Prayer Answered/Confirmed

_____

_____

_____

PRAYER NEED

_____

_____

_____

Scripture

_____

_____

_____

Date Prayer Answered/Confirmed

_____

_____

_____

PRAYER NEED

_____

_____

_____

Scripture

_____

_____

_____

Date Prayer Answered/Confirmed

_____

_____

_____

PRAYER NEED

_____

_____

_____

Scripture

_____

_____

_____

Date Prayer Answered/Confirmed

_____

_____

_____

PRAYER NEED

_____

_____

_____

Scripture

_____

_____

_____

Date Prayer Answered/Confirmed

_____

_____

_____

PRAYER NEED

_____

_____

_____

Scripture

_____

_____

_____

Date Prayer Answered/Confirmed

_____

_____

_____

PRAYER NEED

_____

_____

_____

Scripture

_____

_____

_____

Date Prayer Answered/Confirmed

_____

_____

_____

Ruby W. Smith, B.S., M.S., N.D.

PRAYER NEED

_____

_____

_____

Scripture

_____

_____

_____

Date Prayer Answered/Confirmed

_____

_____

_____

PRAYER NEED

_____

_____

_____

Scripture

_____

_____

_____

Date Prayer Answered/Confirmed

_____

_____

_____

PRAYER NEED

_____

_____

_____

Scripture

_____

_____

_____

Date Prayer Answered/Confirmed

_____

_____

_____

PRAYER NEED

_____

_____

_____

Scripture

_____

_____

_____

Date Prayer Answered/Confirmed

_____

_____

_____

PRAYER NEED

_____

_____

_____

Scripture

_____

_____

_____

Date Prayer Answered/Confirmed

_____

_____

_____

PRAYER NEED

_____

_____

_____

Scripture

_____

_____

_____

Date Prayer Answered/Confirmed

_____

_____

_____

PRAYER NEED

_____

_____

_____

Scripture

_____

_____

_____

Date Prayer Answered/Confirmed

_____

_____

_____

PRAYER NEED

_____

_____

_____

Scripture

_____

_____

_____

Date Prayer Answered/Confirmed

_____

_____

_____

PRAYER NEED

_____

_____

_____

Scripture

_____

_____

_____

Date Prayer Answered/Confirmed

_____

_____

_____

PRAYER NEED

_____

_____

_____

Scripture

_____

_____

_____

Date Prayer Answered/Confirmed

_____

_____

_____

PRAYER NEED

_____

_____

_____

Scripture

_____

_____

_____

Date Prayer Answered/Confirmed

_____

_____

_____

PRAYER NEED

_____

_____

_____

Scripture

_____

_____

_____

Date Prayer Answered/Confirmed

_____

_____

_____

Ruby W. Smith, B.S., M.S., N.D.

PRAYER NEED

_____

_____

_____

Scripture

_____

_____

_____

Date Prayer Answered/Confirmed

_____

_____

_____

PRAYER NEED

_____

_____

_____

Scripture

_____

_____

_____

Date Prayer Answered/Confirmed

_____

_____

_____

PRAYER NEED

_____

_____

_____

Scripture

_____

_____

_____

Date Prayer Answered/Confirmed

_____

_____

_____

PRAYER NEED

_____

_____

_____

Scripture

_____

_____

_____

Date Prayer Answered/Confirmed

_____

_____

_____

PRAYER NEED

_____

_____

_____

Scripture

_____

_____

_____

Date Prayer Answered/Confirmed

_____

_____

_____

PRAYER NEED

_____

_____

_____

Scripture

_____

_____

_____

Date Prayer Answered/Confirmed

_____

_____

_____

PRAYER NEED

_____

_____

_____

Scripture

_____

_____

_____

Date Prayer Answered/Confirmed

_____

_____

_____

PRAYER NEED

_____

_____

_____

Scripture

_____

_____

_____

Date Prayer Answered/Confirmed

_____

_____

_____

PRAYER NEED

_____

_____

_____

Scripture

_____

_____

_____

Date Prayer Answered/Confirmed

_____

_____

_____

PRAYER NEED

_____

_____

_____

Scripture

_____

_____

_____

Date Prayer Answered/Confirmed

_____

_____

_____

PRAYER NEED

_____

_____

_____

Scripture

_____

_____

_____

Date Prayer Answered/Confirmed

_____

_____

_____

PRAYER NEED

_____

_____

_____

Scripture

_____

_____

_____

Date Prayer Answered/Confirmed

_____

_____

_____

PRAYER NEED

_____

_____

_____

Scripture

_____

_____

_____

Date Prayer Answered/Confirmed

_____

_____

_____

PRAYER NEED

_____

_____

_____

Scripture

_____

_____

_____

Date Prayer Answered/Confirmed

_____

_____

_____

PRAYER NEED

_____

_____

_____

Scripture

_____

_____

_____

Date Prayer Answered/Confirmed

_____

_____

_____

PRAYER NEED

_____

_____

_____

Scripture

_____

_____

_____

Date Prayer Answered/Confirmed

_____

_____

_____

PRAYER NEED

_____

_____

_____

Scripture

_____

_____

_____

Date Prayer Answered/Confirmed

_____

_____

_____

PRAYER NEED

_____

_____

_____

Scripture

_____

_____

_____

Date Prayer Answered/Confirmed

_____

_____

_____

PRAYER NEED

_____

_____

_____

Scripture

_____

_____

_____

Date Prayer Answered/Confirmed

_____

_____

_____

PRAYER NEED

_____

_____

_____

Scripture

_____

_____

_____

Date Prayer Answered/Confirmed

_____

_____

_____

Ruby W. Smith, B.S., M.S., N.D.

PRAYER NEED

_____

_____

_____

Scripture

_____

_____

_____

Date Prayer Answered/Confirmed

_____

_____

_____

PRAYER NEED

_____

_____

_____

Scripture

_____

_____

_____

Date Prayer Answered/Confirmed

_____

_____

_____

PRAYER NEED

_____

_____

_____

Scripture

_____

_____

_____

Date Prayer Answered/Confirmed

_____

_____

_____

PRAYER NEED

_____

_____

_____

Scripture

_____

_____

_____

Date Prayer Answered/Confirmed

_____

_____

_____

PRAYER NEED

_____

_____

_____

Scripture

_____

_____

_____

Date Prayer Answered/Confirmed

_____

_____

_____

PRAYER NEED

_____

_____

_____

Scripture

_____

_____

_____

Date Prayer Answered/Confirmed

_____

_____

_____

PRAYER NEED

_____

_____

_____

Scripture

_____

_____

_____

Date Prayer Answered/Confirmed

_____

_____

_____

PRAYER NEED

_____

_____

_____

Scripture

_____

_____

_____

Date Prayer Answered/Confirmed

_____

_____

_____

Ruby W. Smith, B.S., M.S., N.D.

PRAYER NEED

_____

_____

_____

Scripture

_____

_____

_____

Date Prayer Answered/Confirmed

_____

_____

_____

PRAYER NEED

_____

_____

_____

Scripture

_____

_____

_____

Date Prayer Answered/Confirmed

_____

_____

_____

PRAYER NEED

_____

_____

_____

Scripture

_____

_____

_____

Date Prayer Answered/Confirmed

_____

_____

_____

PRAYER NEED

_____

_____

_____

Scripture

_____

_____

_____

Date Prayer Answered/Confirmed

_____

_____

_____

Ruby W. Smith, B.S., M.S., N.D.

PRAYER NEED

_____

_____

_____

Scripture

_____

_____

_____

Date Prayer Answered/Confirmed

_____

_____

_____

PRAYER NEED

_____

_____

_____

Scripture

_____

_____

_____

Date Prayer Answered/Confirmed

_____

_____

_____

PRAYER NEED

_____

_____

_____

Scripture

_____

_____

_____

Date Prayer Answered/Confirmed

_____

_____

_____

PRAYER NEED

_____

_____

_____

Scripture

_____

_____

_____

Date Prayer Answered/Confirmed

_____

_____

_____

PRAYER NEED

_____

_____

_____

Scripture

_____

_____

_____

Date Prayer Answered/Confirmed

_____

_____

_____

PRAYER NEED

_____

_____

_____

Scripture

_____

_____

_____

Date Prayer Answered/Confirmed

_____

_____

_____

PRAYER NEED

_____
_____
_____

Scripture

_____
_____
_____

Date Prayer Answered/Confirmed

_____
_____
_____

PRAYER NEED

_____
_____
_____

Scripture

_____
_____
_____

Date Prayer Answered/Confirmed

_____
_____
_____

PRAYER NEED

_____

_____

_____

Scripture

_____

_____

_____

Date Prayer Answered/Confirmed

_____

_____

_____

PRAYER NEED

_____

_____

_____

Scripture

_____

_____

_____

Date Prayer Answered/Confirmed

_____

_____

_____

PRAYER NEED

_____

_____

_____

Scripture

_____

_____

_____

Date Prayer Answered/Confirmed

_____

_____

_____

PRAYER NEED

_____

_____

_____

Scripture

_____

_____

_____

Date Prayer Answered/Confirmed

_____

_____

_____

PRAYER NEED

_____

_____

_____

Scripture

_____

_____

_____

Date Prayer Answered/Confirmed

_____

_____

_____

PRAYER NEED

_____

_____

_____

Scripture

_____

_____

_____

Date Prayer Answered/Confirmed

_____

_____

_____

PRAYER NEED

_____

_____

_____

Scripture

_____

_____

_____

Date Prayer Answered/Confirmed

_____

_____

_____

PRAYER NEED

_____

_____

_____

Scripture

_____

_____

_____

Date Prayer Answered/Confirmed

_____

_____

_____

PRAYER NEED

_____

_____

_____

Scripture

_____

_____

_____

Date Prayer Answered/Confirmed

_____

_____

_____

PRAYER NEED

_____

_____

_____

Scripture

_____

_____

_____

Date Prayer Answered/Confirmed

_____

_____

_____

PRAYER NEED

_____

_____

_____

Scripture

_____

_____

_____

Date Prayer Answered/Confirmed

_____

_____

_____

PRAYER NEED

_____

_____

_____

Scripture

_____

_____

_____

Date Prayer Answered/Confirmed

_____

_____

_____

Ruby W. Smith, B.S., M.S., N.D.

PRAYER NEED

_____

_____

_____

Scripture

_____

_____

_____

Date Prayer Answered/Confirmed

_____

_____

_____

PRAYER NEED

_____

_____

_____

Scripture

_____

_____

_____

Date Prayer Answered/Confirmed

_____

_____

_____

PRAYER NEED

_____

_____

_____

Scripture

_____

_____

_____

Date Prayer Answered/Confirmed

_____

_____

_____

PRAYER NEED

_____

_____

_____

Scripture

_____

_____

_____

Date Prayer Answered/Confirmed

_____

_____

_____

PRAYER NEED

_____

_____

_____

Scripture

_____

_____

_____

Date Prayer Answered/Confirmed

_____

_____

_____

PRAYER NEED

_____

_____

_____

Scripture

_____

_____

_____

Date Prayer Answered/Confirmed

_____

_____

_____

PRAYER NEED

_____

_____

_____

Scripture

_____

_____

_____

Date Prayer Answered/Confirmed

_____

_____

_____

PRAYER NEED

_____

_____

_____

Scripture

_____

_____

_____

Date Prayer Answered/Confirmed

_____

_____

_____

PRAYER NEED

_____

_____

_____

Scripture

_____

_____

_____

Date Prayer Answered/Confirmed

_____

_____

_____

PRAYER NEED

_____

_____

_____

Scripture

_____

_____

_____

Date Prayer Answered/Confirmed

_____

_____

_____

PRAYER NEED

_____

_____

_____

Scripture

_____

_____

_____

Date Prayer Answered/Confirmed

_____

_____

_____

PRAYER NEED

_____

_____

_____

Scripture

_____

_____

_____

Date Prayer Answered/Confirmed

_____

_____

_____

PRAYER NEED

_____

_____

_____

Scripture

_____

_____

_____

Date Prayer Answered/Confirmed

_____

_____

_____

PRAYER NEED

_____

_____

_____

Scripture

_____

_____

_____

Date Prayer Answered/Confirmed

_____

_____

_____

PRAYER NEED

_____
_____
_____

Scripture

_____
_____
_____

Date Prayer Answered/Confirmed

_____
_____
_____

PRAYER NEED

_____
_____
_____

Scripture

_____
_____
_____

Date Prayer Answered/Confirmed

_____
_____
_____

PRAYER NEED

_____

_____

_____

Scripture

_____

_____

_____

Date Prayer Answered/Confirmed

_____

_____

_____

PRAYER NEED

_____

_____

_____

Scripture

_____

_____

_____

Date Prayer Answered/Confirmed

_____

_____

_____

PRAYER NEED

_____

_____

_____

Scripture

_____

_____

_____

Date Prayer Answered/Confirmed

_____

_____

_____

PRAYER NEED

_____

_____

_____

Scripture

_____

_____

_____

Date Prayer Answered/Confirmed

_____

_____

_____

Ruby W. Smith, B.S., M.S., N.D.

PRAYER NEED

_____

_____

_____

Scripture

_____

_____

_____

Date Prayer Answered/Confirmed

_____

_____

_____

PRAYER NEED

_____

_____

_____

Scripture

_____

_____

_____

Date Prayer Answered/Confirmed

_____

_____

_____

PRAYER NEED

_____

_____

_____

Scripture

_____

_____

_____

Date Prayer Answered/Confirmed

_____

_____

_____

PRAYER NEED

_____

_____

_____

Scripture

_____

_____

_____

Date Prayer Answered/Confirmed

_____

_____

_____

PRAYER NEED

_____

_____

_____

Scripture

_____

_____

_____

Date Prayer Answered/Confirmed

_____

_____

_____

PRAYER NEED

_____

_____

_____

Scripture

_____

_____

_____

Date Prayer Answered/Confirmed

_____

_____

_____

PRAYER NEED

_____

_____

_____

Scripture

_____

_____

_____

Date Prayer Answered/Confirmed

_____

_____

_____

PRAYER NEED

_____

_____

_____

Scripture

_____

_____

_____

Date Prayer Answered/Confirmed

_____

_____

_____

PRAYER NEED

_____

_____

_____

Scripture

_____

_____

_____

Date Prayer Answered/Confirmed

_____

_____

_____

PRAYER NEED

_____

_____

_____

Scripture

_____

_____

_____

Date Prayer Answered/Confirmed

_____

_____

_____

PRAYER NEED

_____

_____

_____

Scripture

_____

_____

_____

Date Prayer Answered/Confirmed

_____

_____

_____

PRAYER NEED

_____

_____

_____

Scripture

_____

_____

Date Prayer Answered/Confirmed

_____

_____

_____

Ruby W. Smith, B.S., M.S., N.D.

PRAYER NEED

_____

_____

_____

Scripture

_____

_____

_____

Date Prayer Answered/Confirmed

_____

_____

_____

PRAYER NEED

_____

_____

_____

Scripture

_____

_____

_____

Date Prayer Answered/Confirmed

_____

_____

_____

PRAYER NEED

_____
_____
_____

Scripture

_____
_____
_____

Date Prayer Answered/Confirmed

_____
_____
_____

PRAYER NEED

_____
_____
_____

Scripture

_____
_____
_____

Date Prayer Answered/Confirmed

_____
_____
_____

PRAYER NEED

_____

_____

_____

Scripture

_____

_____

_____

Date Prayer Answered/Confirmed

_____

_____

_____

PRAYER NEED

_____

_____

_____

Scripture

_____

_____

_____

Date Prayer Answered/Confirmed

_____

_____

_____

PRAYER NEED

_____

_____

_____

Scripture

_____

_____

_____

Date Prayer Answered/Confirmed

_____

_____

_____

PRAYER NEED

_____

_____

_____

Scripture

_____

_____

_____

Date Prayer Answered/Confirmed

_____

_____

_____

PRAYER NEED

_____

_____

_____

Scripture

_____

_____

_____

Date Prayer Answered/Confirmed

_____

_____

_____

PRAYER NEED

_____

_____

_____

Scripture

_____

_____

_____

Date Prayer Answered/Confirmed

_____

_____

_____

PRAYER NEED

_____

_____

_____

Scripture

_____

_____

_____

Date Prayer Answered/Confirmed

_____

_____

_____

PRAYER NEED

_____

_____

_____

Scripture

_____

_____

_____

Date Prayer Answered/Confirmed

_____

_____

_____

PRAYER NEED

_____

_____

_____

Scripture

_____

_____

_____

Date Prayer Answered/Confirmed

_____

_____

_____

PRAYER NEED

_____

_____

_____

Scripture

_____

_____

_____

Date Prayer Answered/Confirmed

_____

_____

_____

PRAYER NEED

_____

_____

_____

Scripture

_____

_____

_____

Date Prayer Answered/Confirmed

_____

_____

_____

PRAYER NEED

_____

_____

_____

Scripture

_____

_____

_____

Date Prayer Answered/Confirmed

_____

_____

_____

PRAYER NEED

_____

_____

_____

Scripture

_____

_____

_____

Date Prayer Answered/Confirmed

_____

_____

_____

PRAYER NEED

_____

_____

_____

Scripture

_____

_____

_____

Date Prayer Answered/Confirmed

_____

_____

_____

PRAYER NEED

_____

_____

_____

Scripture

_____

_____

_____

Date Prayer Answered/Confirmed

_____

_____

_____

PRAYER NEED

_____

_____

_____

Scripture

_____

_____

_____

Date Prayer Answered/Confirmed

_____

_____

_____

PRAYER NEED

_____

_____

_____

Scripture

_____

_____

_____

Date Prayer Answered/Confirmed

_____

_____

_____

PRAYER NEED

_____

_____

_____

Scripture

_____

_____

_____

Date Prayer Answered/Confirmed

_____

_____

_____

PRAYER NEED

_____

_____

_____

Scripture

_____

_____

_____

Date Prayer Answered/Confirmed

_____

_____

_____

PRAYER NEED

_____

_____

_____

Scripture

_____

_____

_____

Date Prayer Answered/Confirmed

_____

_____

_____

Ruby W. Smith, B.S., M.S., N.D.

PRAYER NEED

_____

_____

_____

Scripture

_____

_____

_____

Date Prayer Answered/Confirmed

_____

_____

_____

PRAYER NEED

_____

_____

_____

Scripture

_____

_____

_____

Date Prayer Answered/Confirmed

_____

_____

_____

PRAYER NEED

_____

_____

_____

Scripture

_____

_____

_____

Date Prayer Answered/Confirmed

_____

_____

_____

PRAYER NEED

_____

_____

_____

Scripture

_____

_____

_____

Date Prayer Answered/Confirmed

_____

_____

_____

PRAYER NEED

_____

_____

_____

Scripture

_____

_____

_____

Date Prayer Answered/Confirmed

_____

_____

_____

PRAYER NEED

_____

_____

_____

Scripture

_____

_____

_____

Date Prayer Answered/Confirmed

_____

_____

_____

PRAYER NEED

_____

_____

_____

Scripture

_____

_____

_____

Date Prayer Answered/Confirmed

_____

_____

_____

PRAYER NEED

_____

_____

_____

Scripture

_____

_____

_____

Date Prayer Answered/Confirmed

_____

_____

_____

PRAYER NEED

_____

_____

_____

Scripture

_____

_____

_____

Date Prayer Answered/Confirmed

_____

_____

_____

PRAYER NEED

_____

_____

_____

Scripture

_____

_____

_____

Date Prayer Answered/Confirmed

_____

_____

_____

Divine Intercessory Prayers

Thankfulness

Corinthians 10:30 If I partake with **thankfulness**, why am I denounced because of that Rom 14:6; 1Tim 4:3,4 for which I give thanks?

Colossians 3:16 Let [John 15:3] the word of Christ dwell in you richly, teaching and admonishing one another in all wisdom, [Eph 5:19] singing psalms and hymns and spiritual songs, [Colossians 4:6] with **thankfulness** in your hearts to God.

When Childless
Genesis 15:1, 2, 3

¹After these things the word of the LORD came unto Abram in a vision, saying, Fear not, Abram: I am thy shield, and thy exceeding great reward.

²And Abram said, LORD God, what wilt thou give me, seeing I go childless, and the steward of my house is this Eliezer of Damascus?

³And Abram said, Behold, to me thou hast given no seed: and, lo, one born in my house * I Sam 1:10, 11

¹⁰And she was in bitterness of soul, and prayed unto the LORD, and wept sore.

¹¹And she vowed a vow, and said, O LORD of hosts, if thou wilt indeed look on the affliction of thine handmaid, and remember me, and not forget thine handmaid, but wilt give unto thine handmaid a man child, then I

will give him unto the LORD all the days of his life, and there shall no razor come upon his head.

In Guidance in training an unborn child
Judges 13:2-8

²And there was a certain man of Zorah, of the family of the Danites, whose name was Manoah; and his wife was barren, and bare not.

³And the angel of the LORD appeared unto the woman, and said unto her, Behold now, thou art barren, and bearest not: but thou shalt conceive, and bear a son.

⁴Now therefore beware, I pray thee, and drink not wine nor strong drink, and eat not any unclean thing:

⁵For, lo, thou shalt conceive, and bear a son; and no razor shall come on his head: for the child shall be a Nazarite unto God from the womb: and he shall begin to deliver Israel out of the hand of the Philistines.

⁶Then the woman came and told her husband, saying, A man of God came unto me, and his countenance was like the countenance of an angel of God, very terrible: but I asked him not whence he was, neither told he me his name:

⁷But he said unto me, Behold, thou shalt conceive, and bear a son; and now drink no wine nor strong drink, neither eat any unclean thing: for the child shall be a Nazarite to God from the womb to the day of his death.

⁸Then Manoah intreated the LORD, and said, O my Lord, let the man of God which thou didst send come again unto us, and teach us what we shall do unto the child that shall be born.

In Guidance in training an unborn child
Judges 13:2-8

²And there was a certain man of Zorah, of the family of the Danites, whose name was Manoah; and his wife was barren, and bare not.

³And the angel of the LORD appeared unto the woman, and said unto her, Behold now, thou art barren, and bearest not: but thou shalt conceive, and bear a son.

⁴Now therefore beware, I pray thee, and drink not wine nor strong drink, and eat not any unclean thing:

⁵For, lo, thou shalt conceive, and bear a son; and no razor shall come on his head: for the child shall be a Nazarite unto God from the womb: and he shall begin to deliver Israel out of the hand of the Philistines.

⁶Then the woman came and told her husband, saying, A man of God came unto me, and his countenance was like the countenance of an angel of God, very terrible: but I asked him not whence he was, neither told he me his name:

⁷But he said unto me, Behold, thou shalt conceive, and bear a son; and now drink no wine nor strong drink, neither eat any unclean thing: for the child shall be a Nazarite to God from the womb to the day of his death.

⁸Then Manoah intreated the LORD, and said, O my Lord, let the man of God which thou didst send come again unto us, and teach us what we shall do unto the child that shall be born.

Overwhelmed by guilt
Psalms 38

¹O Lord, rebuke me not in thy wrath: neither chasten me in thy hot displeasure.

²For thine arrows stick fast in me, and thy hand presseth me sore.

³There is no soundness in my flesh because of thine anger; neither is there any rest in my bones because of my sin.

⁴For mine iniquities are gone over mine head: as an heavy burden they are too heavy for me.

⁵My wounds stink and are corrupt because of my foolishness.

⁶I am troubled; I am bowed down greatly; I go mourning all the day long.

⁷For my loins are filled with a loathsome disease: and there is no soundness in my flesh.

⁸I am feeble and sore broken: I have roared by reason of the disquietness of my heart.

⁹Lord, all my desire is before thee; and my groaning is not hid from thee.

¹⁰My heart panteth, my strength faileth me: as for the light of mine eyes, it also is gone from me.

¹¹My lovers and my friends stand aloof from my sore; and my kinsmen stand afar off.

¹²They also that seek after my life lay snares for me: and they that seek my hurt speak mischievous things, and imagine deceits all the day long.

¹³But I, as a deaf man, heard not; and I was as a dumb man that openeth not his mouth.

¹⁴Thus I was as a man that heareth not, and in whose mouth are no reproofs.

¹⁵For in thee, O LORD, do I hope: thou wilt hear, O Lord my God.

¹⁶For I said, Hear me, lest otherwise they should rejoice over me: when my foot slippeth, they magnify themselves against me.

¹⁷For I am ready to halt, and my sorrow is continually before me.

¹⁸For I will declare mine iniquity; I will be sorry for my sin.

¹⁹But mine enemies are lively, and they are strong: and they that hate me wrongfully are multiplied.

²⁰They also that render evil for good are mine adversaries; because I follow the thing that good is.

²¹Forsake me not, O LORD: O my God, be not far from me. 22Make haste to help me, O Lord my salvation.

Sleepless with anxiety
Psalm 77

¹I cried unto God with my voice, even unto God with my voice; and he gave ear unto me.

²In the day of my trouble I sought the Lord: my sore ran in the night, and ceased not: my soul refused to be comforted.

³I remembered God, and was troubled: I complained, and my spirit was overwhelmed. Selah.

⁴Thou holdest mine eyes waking: I am so troubled that I cannot speak.

⁵I have considered the days of old, the years of ancient times.

⁶I call to remembrance my song in the night: I commune with mine own heart: and my spirit made diligent search.

⁷Will the Lord cast off for ever? and will he be favourable no more?

⁸Is his mercy clean gone for ever? doth his promise fail for evermore?

[9]Hath God forgotten to be gracious? hath he in anger shut up his tender mercies? Selah.

[10]And I said, This is my infirmity: but I will remember the years of the right hand of the most High.

[11]I will remember the works of the LORD: surely I will remember thy wonders of old.

[12]I will meditate also of all thy work, and talk of thy doings.

[13]Thy way, O God, is in the sanctuary: who is so great a God as our God?

[14]Thou art the God that doest wonders: thou hast declared thy strength among the people.

[15]Thou hast with thine arm redeemed thy people, the sons of Jacob and Joseph. Selah.

[16]The waters saw thee, O God, the waters saw thee; they were afraid: the depths also were troubled.

[17]The clouds poured out water: the skies sent out a sound: thine arrows also went abroad.

[18]The voice of thy thunder was in the heaven: the lightnings lightened the world: the earth trembled and shook.

[19]Thy way is in the sea, and thy path in the great waters, and thy footsteps are not known.

[20]Thou leddest thy people like a flock by the hand of Moses and Aaron.

When bottom drops out
Psalms 11

¹In the LORD put I my trust: how say ye to my soul, Flee as a bird to your mountain?

²For, lo, the wicked bend their bow, they make ready their arrow upon the string, that they may privily shoot at the upright in heart.

³If the foundations be destroyed, what can the righteous do?

⁴The LORD is in his holy temple, the LORD's throne is in heaven: his eyes behold, his eyelids try, the children of men.

⁵The LORD trieth the righteous: but the wicked and him that loveth violence his soul hateth.

⁶Upon the wicked he shall rain snares, fire and brimstone, and an horrible tempest: this shall be the portion of their cup.

⁷For the righteous LORD loveth righteousness; his countenance doth behold the upright

Genesis 17:17,18

¹⁷Then Abraham fell upon his face, and laughed, and said in his heart, Shall a child be born unto him that is an hundred years old? and shall Sarah, that is ninety years old, bear?

¹⁸And Abraham said unto God, O that Ishmael might live before thee!

Deliverance
Jonah 2

¹Then Jonah prayed unto the LORD his God out of the fish's belly,

²And said, I cried by reason of mine affliction unto the LORD, and he heard me; out of the belly of hell cried I, and thou heardest my voice.

³For thou hadst cast me into the deep, in the midst of the seas; and the floods compassed me about: all thy billows and thy waves passed over me.

⁴Then I said, I am cast out of thy sight; yet I will look again toward thy holy temple.

⁵The waters compassed me about, even to the soul: the depth closed me round about, the weeds were wrapped about my head.

⁶I went down to the bottoms of the mountains; the earth with her bars was about me for ever: yet hast thou brought up my life from corruption, O LORD my God.

⁷When my soul fainted within me I remembered the LORD: and my prayer came in unto thee, into thine holy temple.

⁸They that observe lying vanities forsake their own mercy.

⁹But I will sacrifice unto thee with the voice of thanksgiving; I will pay that that I have vowed. Salvation is of the LORD.

¹⁰And the LORD spake unto the fish, and it vomited out Jonah upon the dry land.

When impossible situation
Psalms 57

¹Be merciful unto me, O God, be merciful unto me: for my soul trusteth in thee: yea, in the shadow of thy wings will I make my refuge, until these calamities be overpast.

²I will cry unto God most high; unto God that performeth all things2I will cry unto God most high; unto God that performeth all things for me.

³He shall send from heaven, and save me from the reproach of him that would swallow me up. Selah. God shall send forth his mercy and his truth.

⁴My soul is among lions: and I lie even among them that are set on fire, even the sons of men, whose teeth are spears and arrows, and their tongue a sharp sword.

⁵Be thou exalted, O God, above the heavens; let thy glory be above all the earth.

⁶They have prepared a net for my steps; my soul is bowed down: they have digged a pit before me, into the midst whereof they are fallen themselves. Selah.

⁷My heart is fixed, O God, my heart is fixed: I will sing and give praise. 8Awake up, my glory; awake, psaltery and harp: I myself will awake early. 9I will praise thee, O Lord, among the people: I will sing unto thee among the nations. 10For thy mercy is great unto the heavens, and thy truth unto the clouds. 11Be thou exalted, O God, above the heavens: let thy glory be above all the earth.

Intercessory for the people
Ezekiel 9:8

And it came to pass, while they were slaying them, and I was left, that I fell upon my face, and cried, and said, Ah Lord GOD! wilt thou destroy all the residue of Israel in thy pouring out of thy fury upon Jerusalem?

Exodus 32:11-14

¹¹ But Moses tried to pacify the Lord his God. "O Lord!" he said. "Why are you so angry with your own people whom you brought from the land of Egypt with such great power and such a strong hand?

¹² Why let the Egyptians say, 'Their God rescued them with the evil intention of slaughtering them in the mountains and wiping them from

the face of the earth'? Turn away from your fierce anger. Change your mind about this terrible disaster you have threatened against your people!

[13] Remember your servants Abraham, Isaac, and Jacob. You bound yourself with an oath to them, saying, "I will make your descendants as numerous as the stars of heaven. And I will give them all of this land that I have promised to your descendants, and they will possess it forever."

[14] So the Lord changed his mind about the terrible disaster he had threatened to bring on his people.

2 Samuel 24:17

[17] When David saw the angel, he said to the Lord, "I am the one who has sinned and done wrong! But these people are as innocent as sheep—what have they done? Let your anger fall against me and my family."

In conflict with another

2 Chronicles 14:11 11 Then Asa cried out to the Lord his God, "O Lord, no one but you can help the powerless against the mighty! Help us, O Lord our God, for we trust in you alone. It is in your name that we have come against this vast horde. O Lord, you are our God; do not let mere men prevail against you!"

Prayer for a city/country

Genesis 18:23-32 And the men turned their faces from thence, and went toward Sodom: but Abraham stood yet before the LORD.

Genesis 18:23 And Abraham drew near, and said, Wilt thou also destroy the righteous with the wicked? Genesis 18:24 Peradventure there be fifty righteous within the city: wilt thou also destroy and not spare the place for the fifty righteous that [are] therein? Genesis 18:25 That be far from thee to do after this manner, to slay the righteous with the wicked: and that the righteous should be as the wicked, that be far from thee: Shall not the Judge of all the earth do right?

Genesis 18:26 And the LORD said, If I find in Sodom fifty righteous within the city, then I will spare all the place for their sakes.

Genesis 18:27 And Abraham answered and said, Behold now, I have taken upon me to speak unto the Lord, which [am but] dust and ashes:

Genesis 18:28 Peradventure there shall lack five of the fifty righteous: wilt thou destroy all the city for [lack of] five? And he said, If I find there forty and five, I will not destroy it.

Genesis 18:29 And he spake unto him yet again, and said, Peradventure there shall be forty found there. And he said, I will not do it for forty's sake.

Genesis 18:30 And he said [unto him], Oh let not the Lord be angry, and I will speak: Peradventure there shall thirty be found there. And he said, I will not do it, if I find thirty there.

Genesis 18:31 And he said, Behold now, I have taken upon me to speak unto the Lord: Peradventure there shall be twenty found there. And he said, I will not destroy it for twenty's sake.

Genesis 18:32 And he said, Oh let not the Lord be angry, and I will speak yet but this once: Peradventure ten shall be found there. And he said, I will not destroy it for ten's sake.

Prayer for others (intercessory)
Acts 7:59, 60

[59]And they stoned Stephen, calling upon God, and saying, Lord Jesus, receive my spirit.

[60]And he kneeled down, and cried with a loud voice, Lord, lay not this sin to their charge. And when he had said this, he fell asleep.

2 Samuel 24:17 17And David spake unto the LORD when he saw the angel that smote the people, and said, Lo, I have sinned, and I have done

wickedly: but these sheep, what have they done? let thine hand, I pray thee, be against me, and against my father's house.

Unsantified

2 Chrronicle 30:18 For a multitude of the people, [even] many of Ephraim, and Manasseh, Issachar, and Zebulun, had not cleansed themselves, yet did they eat the passover otherwise than it was written. But Hezekiah prayed for them, saying, The good LORD pardon every one

[2] Chronicles 30:19 That prepareth his heart to seek God, the LORD God of his fathers, though [he be] not [cleansed] according to the purification of the sanctuary

Strengthen faith
Luke 22:31-32

[31]And the Lord said, Simon, Simon, behold, Satan hath desired to have you, that he may sift you as wheat:

[32]But I have prayed for thee, that thy faith fail not: and when thou art converted, strengthen thy brethren.

When seriously ill
[2]Kings20:1-6

[1]In those days was Hezekiah sick unto death. And the prophet Isaiah the son of Amoz came to him, and said unto him, Thus saith the LORD, Set thine house in order; for thou shalt die, and not live.

[2]Then he turned his face to the wall, and prayed unto the LORD, saying,

[3]I beseech thee, O LORD, remember now how I have walked before thee in truth and with a perfect heart, and have done that which is good in thy sight. And Hezekiah wept sore.

⁴And it came to pass, afore Isaiah was gone out into the middle court, that the word of the LORD came to him, saying,

⁵Turn again, and tell Hezekiah the captain of my people, Thus saith the LORD, the God of David thy father, I have heard thy prayer, I have seen thy tears: behold, I will heal thee: on the third day thou shalt go up unto the house of the LORD.

⁶And I will add unto thy days fifteen years; and I will deliver thee and this city out of the hand of the king of Assyria; and I will defend this city for mine own sake, and for my servant David's sake.

For divine mercy
Luke 18:13,14

¹³And the publican, standing afar off, would not lift up so much as his eyes unto heaven, but smote upon his breast, saying, God be merciful to me a sinner.

¹⁴I tell you, this man went down to his house justified rather than the other: for every one that exalteth himself shall be abased; and he that humbleth himself shall be exalted.

Find a wife/husband
Genesis 24:12

¹²And he said O LORD God of my master Abraham, I pray thee, send me good speed this day, and shew kindness unto my master Abraham.

2 Chronicles 20:6-13

⁶And said, O LORD God of our fathers, art not thou God in heaven? and rulest not thou over all the kingdoms of the heathen? and in thine hand is there not power and might, so that none is able to withstand thee?

[7]Art not thou our God, who didst drive out the inhabitants of this land before thy people Israel, and gavest it to the seed of Abraham thy friend for ever?

[8]And they dwelt therein, and have built thee a sanctuary therein for thy name, saying,

[9]If, when evil cometh upon us, as the sword, judgment, or pestilence, or famine, we stand before this house, and in thy presence, (for thy name is in this house,) and cry unto thee in our affliction, then thou wilt hear and help.

[10]And now, behold, the children of Ammon and Moab and mount Seir, whom thou wouldest not let Israel invade, when they came out of the land of Egypt, but they turned from them, and destroyed them not;

[11]Behold, I say, how they reward us, to come to cast us out of thy possession, which thou hast given us to inherit.

[12]O our God, wilt thou not judge them? for we have no might against this great company that cometh against us; neither know we what to do: but our eyes are upon thee.

[13]And all Judah stood before the LORD, with their little ones, their wives, and their children.

Great Danger
2 Kings 19:14-19

[14]And Hezekiah received the letter of the hand of the messengers, and read it: and Hezekiah went up into the house of the LORD, and spread it before the LORD.

[15]And Hezekiah prayed before the LORD, and said, O LORD God of Israel, which dwellest between the cherubims, thou art the God, even thou alone, of all the kingdoms of the earth; thou hast made heaven and earth.

[16]LORD, bow down thine ear, and hear: open, LORD, thine eyes, and see: and hear the words of Sennacherib, which hath sent him to reproach the living God.

[17]Of a truth, LORD, the kings of Assyria have destroyed the nations and their lands,

[18]And have cast their gods into the fire: for they were no gods, but the work of men's hands, wood and stone: therefore they have destroyed them.

[19]Now therefore, O LORD our God, I beseech thee, save thou us out of his hand, that all the kingdoms of the earth may know that thou art the LORD God, even thou only.

When persecuted
Jeremiah.15:15-18

[15]O LORD, thou knowest: remember me, and visit me, and revenge me of my persecutors; take me not away in thy longsuffering: know that for thy sake I have suffered rebuke.

[16]Thy words were found, and I did eat them; and thy word was unto me the joy and rejoicing of mine heart: for I am called by thy name, O LORD God of hosts.

[17]I sat not in the assembly of the mockers, nor rejoiced; I sat alone because of thy hand: for thou hast filled me with indignation.

[18]Why is my pain perpetual, and my wound incurable, which refuseth to be healed? wilt thou be altogether unto me as a liar, and as waters that fail?

Revival of God's work
Habakkuk 3:1-19

[1]A prayer of Habakkuk the prophet upon Shigionoth.

²O LORD, I have heard thy speech, and was afraid: O LORD, revive thy work in the midst of the years, in the midst of the years make known; in wrath remember mercy.

³God came from Teman, and the Holy One from mount Paran. Selah. His glory covered the heavens, and the earth was full of his praise.

⁴And his brightness was as the light; he had horns coming out of his hand: and there was the hiding of his power.

⁵Before him went the pestilence, and burning coals went forth at his feet.

⁶He stood, and measured the earth: he beheld, and drove asunder the nations; and the everlasting mountains were scattered, the perpetual hills did bow: his ways are everlasting.

⁷I saw the tents of Cushan in affliction: and the curtains of the land of Midian did tremble.

⁸Was the LORD displeased against the rivers? was thine anger against the rivers? was thy wrath against the sea, that thou didst ride upon thine horses and thy chariots of salvation?

⁹Thy bow was made quite naked, according to the oaths of the tribes, even thy word. Selah. Thou didst cleave the earth with rivers.

¹⁰The mountains saw thee, and they trembled: the overflowing of the water passed by: the deep uttered his voice, and lifted up his hands on high.

¹¹The sun and moon stood still in their habitation: at the light of thine arrows they went, and at the shining of thy glittering spear.

¹²Thou didst march through the land in indignation, thou didst thresh the heathen in anger.

¹³Thou wentest forth for the salvation of thy people, even for salvation with thine anointed; thou woundedst the head out of the house of the wicked, by discovering the foundation unto the neck. Selah.

¹⁴Thou didst strike through with his staves the head of his villages: they came out as a whirlwind to scatter me: their rejoicing was as to devour the poor secretly.

¹⁵Thou didst walk through the sea with thine horses, through the heap of great waters.

¹⁶When I heard, my belly trembled; my lips quivered at the voice: rottenness entered into my bones, and I trembled in myself, that I might rest in the day of trouble: when he cometh up unto the people, he will invade them with his troops.

¹⁷Although the fig tree shall not blossom, neither shall fruit be in the vines; the labour of the olive shall fail, and the fields shall yield no meat; the flock shall be cut off from the fold, and there shall be no herd in the stalls:

¹⁸Yet I will rejoice in the LORD, I will joy in the God of my salvation.

¹⁹The LORD God is my strength, and he will make my feet like hinds' feet, and he will make me to walk upon mine high places. To the chief singer on my stringed instruments

Forgiveness
Luke 23:42

⁴And he said unto Jesus, Lord, remember me when thou comest into thy kingdom.

Luke 23:34 ³⁴Then said Jesus, Father, forgive them; for they know not what they do. And they parted h s raiment, and cast lots.

Ruby W. Smith, B.S., M.S., N.D.

Prayer for a specific people
*Daniel 9:3-19

[3]And I set my face unto the Lord God, to seek by prayer and supplications, with fasting, and sackcloth, and ashes:

[4]And I prayed unto the LORD my God, and made my confession, and said, O Lord, the great and dreadful God, keeping the covenant and mercy to them that love him, and to them that keep his commandments;

[5]We have sinned, and have committed iniquity, and have done wickedly, and have rebelled, even by departing from thy precepts and from thy judgments:

[6]Neither have we hearkened unto thy servants the prophets, which spake in thy name to our kings, our princes, and our fathers, and to all the people of the land.

[7]O LORD, righteousness belongeth unto thee, but unto us confusion of faces, as at this day; to the men of Judah, and to the inhabitants of Jerusalem, and unto all Israel, that are near, and that are far off, through all the countries whither thou hast driven them, because of their trespass that they have trespassed against thee.

[8]O Lord, to us belongeth confusion of face, to our kings, to our princes, and to our fathers, because we have sinned against thee.

[9]To the Lord our God belong mercies and forgivenesses, though we have rebelled against him;

[10]Neither have we obeyed the voice of the LORD our God, to walk in his laws, which he set before us by his servants the prophets.

[11]Yea, all Israel have transgressed thy law, even by departing, that they might not obey thy voice; therefore the curse is poured upon us, and the oath that is written in the law of Moses the servant of God, because we have sinned against him.

¹²And he hath confirmed his words, which he spake against us, and against our judges that judged us, by bringing upon us a great evil: for under the whole heaven hath not been done as hath been done upon Jerusalem.

¹³As it is written in the law of Moses, all this evil is come upon us: yet made we not our prayer before the LORD our God, that we might turn from our iniquities, and understand thy truth.

¹⁴Therefore hath the LORD watched upon the evil, and brought it upon us: for the LORD our God is righteous in all his works which he doeth: for we obeyed not his voice.

¹⁵And now, O Lord our God, that hast brought thy people forth out of the land of Egypt with a mighty hand, and hast gotten thee renown, as at this day; we have sinned, we have done wickedly.

¹⁶O LORD, according to all thy righteousness, I beseech thee, let thine anger and thy fury be turned away from thy city Jerusalem, thy holy mountain: because for our sins, and for the iniquities of our fathers, Jerusalem and thy people are become a reproach to all that are about us.

¹⁷Now therefore, O our God, hear the prayer of thy servant, and his supplications, and cause thy face to shine upon thy sanctuary that is desolate, for the Lord's sake.

¹⁸O my God, incline thine ear, and hear; open thine eyes, and behold our desolations, and the city which is called by thy name: for we do not present our supplications before thee for our righteousnesses, but for thy great mercies.

¹⁹O Lord, hear; O Lord, forgive; O Lord, hearken and do; defer not, for thine own sake, O my God: for thy city and thy people are called by thy name.

Wrestling with a divine spirit
Genesis 32:24-30

²⁴And Jacob was left alone; and there wrestled a man with him until the breaking of the day.

²⁵And when he saw that he prevailed not against him, he touched the hollow of his thigh; and the hollow of Jacob's thigh was out of joint, as he wrestled with him.

²⁶And he said, Let me go, for the day breaketh. And he said, I will not let thee go, except thou bless me.

²⁷And he said unto him, What is thy name? And he said, Jacob.

²⁸And he said, Thy name shall be called no more Jacob, but Israel: for as a prince hast thou power with God and with men, and hast prevailed.

²⁹And Jacob asked him, and said, Tell me, I pray thee, thy name. And he said, Wherefore is it that thou dost ask after my name? And he blessed him there.

³⁰And Jacob called the name of the place Peniel: for I have seen God face to face, and my life is preserved.

Gen. 32:9-12 9And Jacob said, O God of my father Abraham, and God of my father Isaac, the LORD

which saidst unto me, Return unto thy country, and to thy kindred, and I will deal well with thee:

¹⁰I am not worthy of the least of all the mercies, and of all the truth, which thou hast shewed unto thy servant; for with my staff I passed over this Jordan; and now I am become two bands.

¹¹Deliver me, I pray thee, from the hand of my brother, from the hand of Esau: for I fear him, lest he will come and smite me, and the mother with the children.

¹²And thou saidst, I will surely do thee good, and make thy seed as the sand of the sea, which cannot be numbered for multitude.

Divine Intervention Because of Iniquity In Family, or a People.
Ezra 9:5-15

⁵And at the evening sacrifice I arose up from my heaviness; and having rent my garment and my mantle, I fell upon my knees, and spread out my hands unto the LORD my God,

⁶And said, O my God, I am ashamed and blush to lift up my face to thee, my God: for our iniquities are increased over our head, and our trespass is grown up unto the heavens.

⁷Since the days of our fathers have we been in a great trespass unto this day; and for our iniquities have we, our kings, and our priests, been delivered into the hand of the kings of the lands, to the sword, to captivity, and to a spoil, and to confusion of face, as it is this day.

⁸And now for a little space grace hath been shewed from the LORD our God, to leave us a remnant to escape, and to give us a nail in his holy place, that our God may lighten our eyes, and give us a little reviving in our bondage.

⁹For we were bondmen; yet our God hath not forsaken us in our bondage, but hath extended mercy unto us in the sight of the kings of Persia, to give us a reviving, to set up the house of our God, and to repair the desolations thereof, and to give us a wall in Judah and in Jerusalem.

¹⁰And now, O our God, what shall we say after this? for we have forsaken thy commandments.

Ruby W. Smith, B.S., M.S., N.D.

¹¹Which thou hast commanded by thy servants the prophets, saying, The land, unto which ye go to possess it, is an unclean land with the filthiness of the people of the lands, with their abominations, which have filled it from one end to another with their uncleanness.

¹²Now therefore give not your daughters unto their sons, neither take their daughters unto your sons, nor seek their peace or their wealth for ever: that ye may be strong, and eat the good of the land, and leave it for an inheritance to your children for ever.

¹³And after all that is come upon us for our evil deeds, and for our great trespass, seeing that thou our God hast punished us less than our iniquities deserve, and hast given us such deliverance as this;

¹⁴Should we again break thy commandments, and join in affinity with the people of these abominations? wouldest not thou be angry with us till thou hadst consumed us, so that there should be no remnant nor escaping?

¹⁵O LORD God of Israel, thou art righteous: for we remain yet escaped, as it is this day: behold, we are before thee in our trespasses: for we cannot stand before thee because of this.

For Thankfulness
*Luke 18:11,12

¹¹The Pharisee stood and prayed thus with himself, God, I thank thee, that I am not as other men are, extortioners, unjust, adulterers, or even as this publican.

¹²I fast twice in the week, I give tithes of all that I possess.

Thankfulness for things hidden and revealed.
*Matthew 11:25-26

²⁵At that time Jesus answered and said, I thank thee, O Father, Lord of heaven and earth, because thou hast hid these things from the wise and prudent, and hast revealed them unto babes.

²⁶Even so, Father: for so it seemed good in thy sight.

For Repentance
*Neh.9:5-38

⁵Then the Levites, Jeshua, and Kadmiel, Bani, Hashabniah, Sherebiah, Hodijah, Shebaniah, and Pethahiah, said, Stand up and bless the LORD your God for ever and ever: and blessed be thy glorious name, which is exalted above all blessing and praise.

⁶Thou, even thou, art LORD alone; thou hast made heaven, the heaven of heavens, with all their host, the earth, and all things that are therein, the seas, and all that is therein, and thou preservest them all; and the host of heaven worshippeth thee.

⁷Thou art the LORD the God, who didst choose Abram, and broughtest him forth out of Ur of the Chaldees, and gavest him the name of Abraham;

⁸And foundest his heart faithful before thee, and madest a covenant with him to give the land of the Canaanites, the Hittites, the Amorites, and the Perizzites, and the Jebusites, and the Girgashites, to give it, I say, to his seed, and hast performed thy words; for thou art righteous:

⁹And didst see the affliction of our fathers in Egypt, and heardest their cry by the Red sea;

¹⁰And shewedst signs and wonders upon Pharaoh, and on all his servants, and on all the people of his land: for thou knewest that they dealt proudly against them. So didst thou get thee a name, as it is this day.

¹¹And thou didst divide the sea before them, so that they went through the midst of the sea on the dry land; and their persecutors thou threwest into the deeps, as a stone into the mighty waters.

¹²Moreover thou leddest them in the day by a cloudy pillar; and in the night by a pillar of fire, to give them light in the way wherein they should go.

[13]Thou camest down also upon mount Sinai, and spakest with them from heaven, and gavest them right judgments, and true laws, good statutes and commandments:

[14]And madest known unto them thy holy sabbath, and commandedst them precepts, statutes, and laws, by the hand of Moses thy servant:

[15]And gavest them bread from heaven for their hunger, and broughtest forth water for them out of the rock for their thirst, and promisedst them that they should go in to possess the land which thou hadst sworn to give them.

[16]But they and our fathers dealt proudly, and hardened their necks, and hearkened not to thy commandments,

[17]And refused to obey, neither were mindful of thy wonders that thou didst among them; but hardened their necks, and in their rebellion appointed a captain to return to their bondage: but thou art a God ready to pardon, gracious and merciful, slow to anger, and of great kindness, and forsookest them not.

[18]Yea, when they had made them a molten calf, and said, This is thy God that brought thee up out of Egypt, and had wrought great provocations;

[19]Yet thou in thy manifold mercies forsookest them not in the wilderness: the pillar of the cloud departed not from them by day, to lead them in the way; neither the pillar of fire by night, to shew them light, and the way wherein they should go.

[20]Thou gavest also thy good spirit to instruct them, and withheldest not thy manna from their mouth, and gavest them water for their thirst.

[21]Yea, forty years didst thou sustain them in the wilderness, so that they lacked nothing; their clothes waxed not old, and their feet swelled not.

²²Moreover thou gavest them kingdoms and nations, and didst divide them into corners: so they possessed the land of Sihon, and the land of the king of Heshbon, and the land of Og king of Bashan.

²³Their children also multipliedst thou as the stars of heaven, and broughtest them into the land, concerning which thou hadst promised to their fathers, that they should go in to possess it.

²⁴So the children went in and possessed the land, and thou subduedst before them the inhabitants of the land, the Canaanites, and gavest them into their hands, with their kings, and the people of the land, that they might do with them as they would.

²⁵And they took strong cities, and a fat land, and possessed houses full of all goods, wells digged, vineyards, and oliveyards, and fruit trees in abundance: so they did eat, and were filled, and became fat, and delighted themselves in thy great goodness.

²⁶Nevertheless they were disobedient, and rebelled against thee, and cast thy law behind their backs, and slew thy prophets which testified against them to turn them to thee, and they wrought great provocations.

²⁷Therefore thou deliveredst them into the hand of their enemies, who vexed them: and in the time of their trouble, when they cried unto thee, thou heardest them from heaven; and according to thy manifold mercies thou gavest them saviours, who saved them out of the hand of their enemies.

²⁸But after they had rest, they did evil again before thee: therefore leftest thou them in the land of their enemies, so that they had the dominion over them: yet when they returned, and cried unto thee, thou heardest them from heaven; and many times didst thou deliver them according to thy mercies;

²⁹And testifiedst against them, that thou mightest bring them again unto thy law: yet they dealt proudly, and hearkened not unto thy commandments,

but sinned against thy judgments, (which if a man do, he shall live in them and withdrew the shoulder, and hardened their neck, and would not hear.

[30]Yet many years didst thou forbear them, and testifiedst against them by thy spirit in thy prophets: yet would they not give ear: therefore gavest thou them into the hand of the people of the lands.

[31]Nevertheless for thy great mercies' sake thou didst not utterly consume them, nor forsake them; for thou art a gracious and merciful God.

[32]Now therefore, our God, the great, the mighty, and the terrible God, who keepest covenant and mercy, let not all the trouble seem little before thee, that hath come upon us, on our kings, on our princes, and on our priests, and on our prophets, and on our fathers, and on all thy people, since the time of the kings of Assyria unto this day.

[33]Howbeit thou art just in all that is brought upon us; for thou hast done right, but we have done wickedly:

[34]Neither have our kings, our princes, our priests, nor our fathers, kept thy law, nor hearkened unto thy commandments and thy testimonies, wherewith thou didst testify against them.

[35]For they have not served thee in their kingdom, and in thy great goodness that thou gavest them, and in the large and fat land which thou gavest before them, neither turned they from their wicked works.

[36]Behold, we are servants this day, and for the land that thou gavest unto our fathers to eat the fruit thereof and the good thereof, behold, we are servants in it:

[37]And it yieldeth much increase unto the kings whom thou hast set over us because of our sins: also they have dominion over our bodies, and over our cattle, at their pleasure, and we are in great distress.

[38]And because of all this we make a sure covenant, and write it; and our princes, Levites, and priests, seal unto it.

For prayer over the state of things.
Neh.1:5-11

⁵And said, I beseech thee, O LORD God of heaven, the great and terrible God, that keepeth covenant and mercy for them that love him and observe his commandments:

⁶Let thine ear now be attentive, and thine eyes open, that thou mayest hear the prayer of thy servant, which I pray before thee now, day and night, for the children of Israel thy servants, and confess the sins of the children of Israel, which we have sinned against thee: both I and my father's house have sinned.

⁷We have dealt very corruptly against thee, and have not kept the commandments, nor the statutes, nor the judgments, which thou commandedst thy servant Moses.

⁸Remember, I beseech thee, the word that thou commandedst thy servant Moses, saying, If ye transgress, I will scatter you abroad among the nations:

⁹But if ye turn unto me, and keep my commandments, and do them; though there were of you cast out unto the uttermost part of the heaven, yet will I gather them from thence, and will bring them unto the place that I have chosen to set my name there.

¹⁰Now these are thy servants and thy people, whom thou hast redeemed by thy great power, and by thy strong hand.

¹¹O LORD, I beseech thee, let now thine ear be attentive to the prayer of thy servant, and to the prayer of thy servants, who desire to fear thy name: and prosper, I pray thee, thy servant this day, and grant him mercy in the sight of this man. For I was the king's cupbearer.

Victim of Deception
Psalms 12

[1]Help, LORD; for the godly man ceaseth; for the faithful fail from among the children of men.

[2]They speak vanity every one with his neighbour: with flattering lips and with a double heart do they speak.

[3]The LORD shall cut off all flattering lips, and the tongue that speaketh proud things:

[4]Who have said, With our tongue will we prevail; our lips are our own: who is lord over us?

[5]For the oppression of the poor, for the sighing of the needy, now will I arise, saith the LORD; I will set him in safety from him that puffeth at him.

[6]The words of the LORD are pure words: as silver tried in a furnace of earth, purified seven times.

[7]Thou shalt keep them, O LORD, thou shalt preserve them from this generation for ever.

The wicked walk on every side, when the vilest men are exalted.

For Divine Presence and Glory Over Life
Exodus 33:12-23

[12]And Moses said unto the LORD, See, thou sayest unto me, Bring up this people: and thou hast not let me know whom thou wilt send with me. Yet thou hast said, I know thee by name, and thou hast also found grace in my sight.

¹³Now therefore, I pray thee, if I have found grace in thy sight, shew me now thy way, that I may know thee, that I may find grace in thy sight: and consider that this nation is thy people.

¹⁴And he said, My presence shall go with thee, and I will give thee rest.

¹⁵And he said unto him, If thy presence go not with me, carry us not up hence.

¹⁶For wherein shall it be known here that I and thy people have found grace in thy sight? is it not in that thou goest with us? so shall we be separated, I and thy people, from all the people that are upon the face of the earth.

¹⁷And the LORD said unto Moses, I will do this thing also that thou hast spoken: for thou hast found grace in my sight, and I know thee by name.

¹⁸And he said, I beseech thee, shew me thy glory.

¹⁹And he said, I will make all my goodness pass before thee, and I will proclaim the name of the LORD before thee; and will be gracious to whom I will be gracious, and will shew mercy on whom I will shew mercy.

²⁰And he said, Thou canst not see my face: for there shall no man see me, and live.

²¹And the LORD said, Behold, there is a place by me, and thou shalt stand upon a rock:

²²And it shall come to pass, while my glory passeth by, that I will put thee in a clift of the rock, and will cover thee with my hand while I pass by:

²³And I will take away mine hand, and thou shalt see my back parts: but my face shall not be seen.

Encouragement

Josh 7:7-97 And Joshua said, Alas, O LORD God, wherefore hast thou at all brought this people over Jordan, to deliver us into the hand of the Amorites, to destroy us? would to God we had been content, and dwelt on the other side Jordan!

⁸O LORD, what shall I say, when Israel turneth their backs before their enemies!

⁹For the Canaanites and all the inhabitants of the land shall hear of it, and shall environ us round, and cut off our name from the earth: and what wilt thou do unto thy great name?

Divine help

Judges 16:28 ²⁸And Samson called unto the LORD, and said, O Lord God, remember me, I pray thee, and strengthen me, I pray thee, only this once, O God, that I may be at once avenged of the Philistines for my two eyes.

Wisdom Luke 22:41-44

⁴¹And he was withdrawn from them about a stone's cast, and kneeled down, and prayed,

⁴²Saying, Father, if thou be willing, remove this cup from me: nevertheless not my will, but thine, be done.

⁴³And there appeared an angel unto him from heaven, strengthening him.

⁴⁴And being in an agony he prayed more earnestly: and his sweat was as it were great drops of blood falling down to the ground.

Tempted
Psalms 28

¹Unto thee will I cry, O LORD my rock; be not silent to me: lest, if thou be silent to me, I become like them that go down into the pit.

²Hear the voice of my supplications, when I cry unto thee, when I lift up my hands toward thy holy oracle.

³Draw me not away with the wicked, and with the workers of iniquity, which speak peace to their neighbours, but mischief is in their hearts.

⁴Give them according to their deeds, and according to the wickedness of their endeavours: give them after the work of their hands; render to them their desert.

⁵Because they regard not the works of the LORD, nor the operation of his hands, he shall destroy them, and not build them up.

⁶Blessed be the LORD, because he hath heard the voice of my supplications.

⁷The LORD is my strength and my shield; my heart trusted in him, and I am helped: therefore my heart greatly rejoiceth; and with my song will I praise him.

⁸The LORD is their strength, and he is the saving strength of his anointed. 9Save thy people, and bless thine inheritance: feed them also, and lift them up for ever.

Restoration
1Kings 17:20, 21

²⁰And he cried unto the LORD, and said, O LORD my God, hast thou also brought evil upon the widow with whom I sojourn, by slaying her son?

²¹And he stretched himself upon the child three times, and cried unto the LORD, and said, O LORD my God, I pray thee, let this child's soul come into him again.

I Kings 3:5-9

⁵In Gibeon the LORD appeared to Solomon in a dream by night: and God said, Ask

what I shall give thee.

⁶And Solomon said, Thou hast shewed unto thy servant David my father great mercy, according as he walked before thee in truth, and in righteousness, and in uprightness of heart with thee; and thou hast kept for him this great kindness, that thou hast given him a son to sit on his throne, as it is this day.

⁷And now, O LORD my God, thou hast made thy servant king instead of David my father: and I am but a little child: I know not how to go out or come in.

⁸And thy servant is in the midst of thy people which thou hast chosen, a great people, that cannot be numbered nor counted for multitude.

⁹Give therefore thy servant an understanding heart to judge thy people, that I may discern between good and bad: for who is able to judge this thy so great a people?

Restoration

1 Kings 17:20,21 20And he cried unto the LORD, and said, O LORD my God, hast thou also brought evil upon the widow with whom I sojourn, by slaying her son?

²¹And he stretched himself upon the child three times, and cried unto the LORD, and said, O LORD my God, I pray thee, let this child's soul come into him again.

Prayer when grieving
*John11:41,42

⁴¹Then they took away the stone from the place where the dead was laid. And Jesus lifted up his eyes, and said, Father, I thank thee that thou hast heard me.

⁴²And I knew that thou hearest me always: but because of the people which stand by I said it, that they may believe that thou hast sent me.

Divine help
I Kings 18:36,37

³⁶And it came to pass at the time of the offering of the evening sacrifice, that Elijah the prophet came near, and said, LORD God of Abraham, Isaac, and of Israel, let it be known this day that thou art God in Israel, and that I am thy servant, and that I have done all these things at thy word.

³⁷Hear me, O LORD, hear me, that this people may know that thou art the LORD God, and that thou hast turned their heart back again.

Depressed
Psalms 55

¹Give ear to my prayer, O God; and hide not thyself from my supplication.

²Attend unto me, and hear me: I mourn in my complaint, and make a noise;

³Because of the voice of the enemy, because of the oppression of the wicked: for they cast iniquity upon me, and in wrath they hate me.

⁴My heart is sore pained within me: and the terrors of death are fallen upon me. 5Fearfulness and trembling are come upon me, and horror hath overwhelmed me.

⁶And I said, Oh that I had wings like a dove! for then would I fly away, and be at rest.

⁷Lo, then would I wander far off, and remain in the wilderness. Selah.

⁸I would hasten my escape from the windy storm and tempest.

⁹Destroy, O Lord, and divide their tongues: for I have seen violence and strife in the city.

¹⁰Day and night they go about it upon the walls thereof: mischief also and sorrow are in the midst of it.

¹¹Wickedness is in the midst thereof: deceit and guile depart not from her streets.

¹²For it was not an enemy that reproached me; then I could have borne it: neither was it he that hated me that did magnify himself against me; then I would have hid myself from him:

¹³But it was thou, a man mine equal, my guide, and mine acquaintance.

¹⁴We took sweet counsel together, and walked unto the house of God in company.

¹⁵Let death seize upon them, and let them go down quick into hell: for wickedness is in their dwellings, and among them.

¹⁶As for me, I will call upon God; and the LORD shall save me.

¹⁷Evening, and morning, and at noon, will I pray, and cry aloud: and he shall hear my voice.

¹⁸He hath delivered my soul in peace from the battle that was against me: for there were many with me.

[19]God shall hear, and afflict them, even he that abideth of old. Selah. Because they have no changes, therefore they fear not God.

[20]He hath put forth his hands against such as be at peace with him: he hath broken his covenant.

[21]The words of his mouth were smoother than butter, but war was in his heart: his words were softer than oil, yet were they drawn swords.

[22]Cast thy burden upon the LORD, and he shall sustain thee: he shall never suffer the righteous to be moved.

[23]But thou, O God, shalt bring them down into the pit of destruction: bloody and deceitful men shall not live out half their days; but I will trust in thee.

Forgiveness

Ps. 51 [1]Have mercy upon me, O God, according to thy lovingkindness: according unto the multitude of thy tender mercies blot out my transgressions. [2]Wash me throughly from mine iniquity, and cleanse me from my sin. [3]For I acknowledge my transgressions: and my sin is ever before me.

[4]Against thee, thee only, have I sinned, and done this evil in thy sight: that thou mightest be justified when thou speakest, and be clear when thou judgest.

[5]Behold, I was shapen in iniquity; and in sin did my mother conceive me.

[6]Behold, thou desirest truth in the inward parts: and in the hidden part thou shalt make me to know wisdom.

[7]Purge me with hyssop, and I shall be clean: wash me, and I shall be whiter than snow. Make me to hear joy and gladness; that the bones which thou hast broken may rejoice. [9]Hide thy face from my sins, and blot out all

mine iniquities. ¹⁰Create in me a clean heart, O God; and renew a right spirit within me.

¹¹Cast me not away from thy presence; and take not thy holy spirit from me.

¹²Restore unto me the joy of thy salvation; and uphold me with thy free spirit.

¹³Then will I teach transgressors thy ways; and sinners shall be converted unto thee.

¹⁴Deliver me from blood guiltiness, O God, thou God of my salvation: and my tongue shall sing aloud of thy righteousness.

¹⁵O Lord, open thou my lips; and my mouth shall shew forth thy praise.

¹⁶For thou desirest not sacrifice; else would I give it: thou delightest not in burnt offering.

¹⁷The sacrifices of God are a broken spirit: a broken and a contrite heart, O God, thou wilt not despise.

¹⁸Do good in thy good pleasure unto Zion: build thou the walls of Jerusalem.

¹⁹Then shalt thou be pleased with the sacrifices of righteousness.

Dedication
I Kings 8:23-53

²³And he said, LORD God of Israel, there is no God like thee, in heaven above, or on earth beneath, who keepest covenant and mercy with thy servants that walk before thee with all their heart:

²⁴Who hast kept with thy servant David my father that thou promisedst him: thou spakest also with thy mouth, and hast fulfilled it with thine hand, as it is this day.

²⁵Therefore now, LORD God of Israel, keep with thy servant David my father that thou promisedst him, saying, There shall not fail thee a man in my sight to sit on the throne of Israel; so that thy children take heed to their way, that they walk before me as thou hast walked before me.

²⁶And now, O God of Israel, let thy word, I pray thee, be verified, which thou spakest unto thy servant David my father.

²⁷But will God indeed dwell on the earth? behold, the heaven and heaven of heavens cannot contain thee; how much less this house that I have builded?

²⁸Yet have thou respect unto the prayer of thy servant, and to his supplication, O LORD my God, to hearken unto the cry and to the prayer, which thy servant prayeth before thee to day:

²⁹That thine eyes may be open toward this house night and day, even toward the place of which thou hast said, My name shall be there: that thou mayest hearken unto the prayer which thy servant shall make toward this place.

³⁰And hearken thou to the supplication of thy servant, and of thy people Israel, when they shall pray toward this place: and hear thou in heaven thy dwelling place: and when thou hearest, forgive.

³¹If any man trespass against his neighbour, and an oath be laid upon him to cause him to swear, and the oath come before thine altar in this house:

³²Then hear thou in heaven, and do, and judge thy servants, condemning the wicked, to bring his way upon his head; and justifying the righteous, to give him according to his righteousness.

³³When thy people Israel be smitten down before the enemy, because they have sinned against thee, and shall turn again to thee, and confess thy name, and pray, and make supplication unto thee in this house:

³⁴Then hear thou in heaven, and forgive the sin of thy people Israel, and bring them again unto the land which thou gavest unto their fathers.

[35]When heaven is shut up, and there is no rain, because they have sinned against thee; if they pray toward this place, and confess thy name, and turn from their sin, when thou afflictest them:

[36]Then hear thou in heaven, and forgive the sin of thy servants, and of thy people Israel, that thou teach them the good way wherein they should walk, and give rain upon thy land, which thou hast given to thy people for an inheritance.

[37]If there be in the land famine, if there be pestilence, blasting, mildew, locust, or if there be caterpiller; if their enemy besiege them in the land of their cities; whatsoever plague, whatsoever sickness there be;

[38]What prayer and supplication soever be made by any man, or by all thy people Israel, which shall know every man the plague of his own heart, and spread forth his hands toward this house:

[39]Then hear thou in heaven thy dwelling place, and forgive, and do, and give to every man according to his ways, whose heart thou knowest; for thou, even thou only, knowest the hearts of all the children of men;

[40]That they may fear thee all the days that they live in the land which thou gavest unto our fathers.

[41]Moreover concerning a stranger, that is not of thy people Israel, but cometh out of a far country for thy name's sake;

[42](For they shall hear of thy great name, and of thy strong hand, and of thy stretched out arm;) when he shall come and pray toward this house;

[43]Hear thou in heaven thy dwelling place, and do according to all that the stranger calleth to thee for: that all people of the earth may know thy name, to fear thee, as do thy people Israel; and that they may know that this house, which I have builded, is called by thy name.

⁴⁴If thy people go out to battle against their enemy, whithersoever thou shalt send them, and shall pray unto the LORD toward the city which thou hast chosen, and toward the house that I have built for thy name:

⁴⁵Then hear thou in heaven their prayer and their supplication, and maintain their cause.

⁴⁶If they sin against thee, (for there is no man that sinneth not,) and thou be angry with them, and deliver them to the enemy, so that they carry them away captives unto the land of the enemy, far or near;

⁴⁷Yet if they shall bethink themselves in the land whither they were carried captives, and repent, and make supplication unto thee in the land of them that carried them captives, saying, We have sinned, and have done perversely, we have committed wickedness;

⁴⁸And so return unto thee with all their heart, and with all their soul, in the land of their enemies, which led them away captive, and pray unto thee toward their land, which thou gavest unto their fathers, the city which thou hast chosen, and the house which I have built for thy name:

⁴⁹Then hear thou their prayer and their supplication in heaven thy dwelling place, and maintain their cause,

⁵⁰And forgive thy people that have sinned against thee, and all their transgressions wherein they have transgressed against thee, and give them compassion before them who carried them captive, that they may have compassion on them:

⁵¹For they be thy people, and thine inheritance, which thou broughtest forth out of Egypt, from the midst of the furnace of iron:

⁵²That thine eyes may be open unto the supplication of thy servant, and unto the supplication of thy people Israel, to hearken unto them in all that they call for unto thee.

[53]For thou didst separate them from among all the people of the earth, to be thine inheritance, as thou spakest by the hand of Moses thy servant, when thou broughtest our fathers out of Egypt, O LORD God.

I Chronicles 29:10-19

[10]Wherefore David blessed the LORD before all the congregation: and David said, Blessed be thou, LORD God of Israel our father, for ever and ever.

[11]Thine, O LORD is the greatness, and the power, and the glory, and the victory, and the majesty: for all that is in the heaven and in the earth is thine; thine is the kingdom, O LORD, and thou art exalted as head above all.

[12]Both riches and honour come of thee, and thou reignest over all; and in thine hand is power and might; and in thine hand it is to make great, and to give strength unto all.

[13]Now therefore, our God, we thank thee, and praise thy glorious name.

[14]But who am I, and what is my people, that we should be able to offer so willingly after this sort? for all things come of thee, and of thine own have we given thee.

[15]For we are strangers before thee, and sojourners, as were all our fathers: our days on the earth are as a shadow, and there is none abiding.

[16]O LORD our God, all this store that we have prepared to build thee an house for thine holy name cometh of thine hand, and is all thine own.

[17]I know also, my God, that thou triest the heart, and hast pleasure in uprightness. As for me, in the uprightness of mine heart I have willingly offered all these things: and now have I seen with joy thy people, which are present here, to offer willingly unto thee.

¹⁸O LORD God of Abraham, Isaac, and of Israel, our fathers, keep this for ever in the imagination of the thoughts of the heart of thy people, and prepare their heart unto thee:

¹⁹And give unto Solomon my son a perfect heart, to keep thy commandments, thy testimonies, and thy statutes, and to do all these things, and to build the palace, for the which I have made provision.

For a leader
Num.27:15-23

¹⁵And Moses spake unto the LORD, saying,

¹⁶Let the LORD, the God of the spirits of all flesh, set a man over the congregation,

¹⁷Which may go out before them, and which may go in before them, and which may lead them out, and which may bring them in; that the congregation of the LORD be not as sheep which have no shepherd.

¹⁸And the LORD said unto Moses, Take thee Joshua the son of Nun, a man in whom is the spirit, and lay thine hand upon him;

¹⁹And set him before Eleazar the priest, and before all the congregation; and give him a charge in their sight.

²⁰And thou shalt put some of thine honour upon him, that all the congregation of the children of Israel may be obedient.

²¹And he shall stand before Eleazar the priest, who shall ask counsel for him after the judgment of Urim before the LORD: at his word shall they go out, and at his word they shall come in, both he, and all the children of Israel with him, even all the congregation.

²²And Moses did as the LORD commanded him: and he took Joshua, and set him before Eleazar the priest, and before all the congregation:

²³And he laid his hands upon him, and gave him a charge, as the LORD commanded by the hand of Moses.

Intercessory for faithless
Numbers 14:13-19

¹³And Moses said unto the LORD, Then the Egyptians shall hear it, (for thou broughtest up this people in thy might from among them;)

¹⁴And they will tell it to the inhabitants of this land: for they have heard that thou LORD art among this people, that thou LORD art seen face to face, and that thy cloud standeth over them, and that thou goest before them, by day time in a pillar of a cloud, and in a pillar of fire by night.

¹⁵Now if thou shalt kill all this people as one man, then the nations which have heard the fame of thee will speak, saying,

¹⁶Because the LORD was not able to bring this people into the land which he sware unto them, therefore he hath slain them in the wilderness.

¹⁷And now, I beseech thee, let the power of my lord be great, according as thou hast spoken, saying,

¹⁸The LORD is longsuffering, and of great mercy, forgiving iniquity and transgression, and by no means clearing the guilty, visiting the iniquity of the fathers upon the children unto the third and fourth generation.

¹⁹Pardon, I beseech thee, the iniquity of this people according unto the greatness of thy mercy, and as thou hast forgiven this people, from Egypt even until now.

When entering a new place
Deut.3:24,25

²⁴O Lord GOD, thou hast begun to shew thy servant thy greatness, and thy mighty hand: for what God is there in heaven or in earth, that can do according to thy works, and according to thy might?

[25]I pray thee, let me go over, and see the good land that is beyond Jordan, that goodly mountain, and Lebanon.

Prayer on behalf of another who criticizes.
*Numbers 12:13

[13] So Moses cried out to the Lord, "O God, I beg you, please heal her!"

Prayer for being falsely accused
Psalms 7

[1]O LORD my God, in thee do I put my trust: save me from all them that persecute me, and deliver me:

[2]Lest he tear my soul like a lion, rending it in pieces, while there is none to deliver.

[3]O LORD my God, If I have done this; if there be iniquity in my hands;

[4]If I have rewarded evil unto him that was at peace with me; Yes, I have delivered him that without cause is mine enemy.

[5]Let the enemy persecute my soul, and take it; yea, let him tread down my life upon the earth, and lay mine honour in the dust. Selah.

[6]Arise, O LORD, in thine anger, lift up thyself because of the rage of mine enemies: and awake for me to the judgment that thou hast commanded.

[7]So shall the congregation of the people compass thee about: for their sakes therefore return thou on high.

[8]The LORD shall judge the people: judge me, O LORD, according to my righteousness, and according to mine integrity that is in me.

[9]Oh let the wickedness of the wicked come to an end; but establish the just: for the righteous God trieth the hearts and reins.

Ruby W. Smith, B.S., M.S., N.D.

[10]My defence is of God, which saveth the upright in heart.

[11]God judgeth the righteous, and God is angry with the wicked every day.

[12]If he turn not, he will whet his sword; he hath bent his bow, and made it ready.

[13]He hath also prepared for him the instruments of death; he ordaineth his arrows against the persecutors.

[14]Behold, he travaileth with iniquity, and hath conceived mischief, and brought forth falsehood.

[15]He made a pit, and digged it, and is fallen into the ditch which he made.

[16]His mischief shall return upon his own head, and his violent dealing shall come down upon his own pate.

[17]I will praise the LORD according to his righteousness: and will sing praise to the name of the LORD most high.

Lord's Prayer
Matt.6:9-15

[9]After this manner therefore pray ye: Our Father which art in heaven, Hallowed be thy name.

[10]Thy kingdom come, Thy will be done in earth, as it is in heaven.

[11]Give us this day our daily bread.

[12]And forgive us our debts, as we forgive our debtors.

[13]And lead us not into temptation, but deliver us from evil: For thine is the kingdom, and the power, and the glory, for ever. Amen.

¹⁴For if ye forgive men their trespasses, your heavenly Father will also forgive you:

¹⁵But if ye forgive not men their trespasses, neither will your Father forgive your trespasses.

Prayer for Christ's Return
*Revelation 22:20

²⁰ He who is the faithful witness to all these things says, "Yes, I am coming soon!"

Prayer when lonely

Psalms 42 ¹As the hart panteth after the water brooks, so panteth my soul after thee, O God.

²My soul thirsteth for God, for the living God: when shall I come and appear before God?

³My tears have been my meat day and night, while they continually say unto me, Where is thy God?

⁴When I remember these things, I pour out my soul in me: for I had gone with the multitude, I went with them to the house of God, with the voice of joy and praise, with a multitude that kept holyday.

⁵Why art thou cast down, O my soul? and why art thou disquieted in me? hope thou in God: for I shall yet praise him for the help of his countenance.

⁶O my God, my soul is cast down within me: therefore will I remember thee from the land of Jordan, and of the Hermonites, from the hill Mizar.

⁷Deep calleth unto deep at the noise of thy waterspouts: all thy waves and thy billows are gone over me.

Ruby W. Smith, B.S., M.S., N.D.

⁸Yet the LORD will command his lovingkindness in the day time, and in the night his song shall be with me, and my prayer unto the God of my life.

⁹I will say unto God my rock, Why hast thou forgotten me? why go I mourning because of the oppression of the enemy?

¹⁰As with a sword in my bones, mine enemies reproach me; while they say daily unto me, Where is thy God?

¹¹Why art thou cast down, O my soul? and why art thou disquieted within me? hope thou in God: for I shall yet praise him, who is the health of my countenance, and my God.

Distress
Psalms 6

¹O LORD, rebuke me not in thine anger, neither chasten me in thy hot displeasure.

²Have mercy upon me, O LORD; for I am weak: O LORD, heal me; for my bones are vexed.

³My soul is also sore vexed: but thou, O LORD, how long?

⁴Return, O LORD, deliver my soul: oh save me for thy mercies' sake.

⁵For in death there is no remembrance of thee: in the grave who shall give thee thanks?

⁶I am weary with my groaning; all the night make I my bed to swim; I water my couch with my tears.

⁷Mine eye is consumed because of grief; it waxeth old because of all mine enemies.

⁸Depart from me, all ye workers of iniquity; for the LORD hath heard the voice of my weeping.

⁹The LORD hath heard my supplication; the LORD will receive my prayer.

¹⁰Let all mine enemies be ashamed and sore vexed: let them return and be ashamed suddenly.

Psalms 13

¹How long wilt thou forget me, O LORD? for ever? how long wilt thou hide thy face from me?

²How long shall I take counsel in my soul, having sorrow in my heart daily? how long shall mine enemy be exalted over me?

³Consider and hear me, O LORD my God: lighten mine eyes, lest I sleep the sleep of death;

⁴Lest mine enemy say, I have prevailed against him; and those that trouble me rejoice when I am moved.

⁵But I have trusted in thy mercy; my heart shall rejoice in thy salvation.

⁶I will sing unto the LORD, because he hath dealt bountifully with me.

When Afraid
Psalms 56

Be merciful unto me, O God: for man would swallow me up; he fighting daily oppresseth me.

²Mine enemies would daily swallow me up: for they be many that fight against me, O thou most High.

³What time I am afraid, I will trust in thee.

⁴In God I will praise his word, in God I have put my trust; I will not fear what flesh can do unto me.

⁵Every day they wrest my words: all their thoughts are against me for evil.

⁶They gather themselves together, they hide themselves, they mark my steps, when they wait for my soul.

⁷Shall they escape by iniquity? in thine anger cast down the people, O God.

⁸Thou tellest my wanderings: put thou my tears into thy bottle: are they not in thy book?

⁹When I cry unto thee, then shall mine enemies turn back: this I know; for God is for me.

¹⁰In God will I praise his word: in the LORD will I praise his word.

¹¹In God have I put my trust: I will not be afraid what man can do unto me.

¹²Thy vows are upon me, O God: I will render praises unto thee.

¹³For thou hast delivered my soul from death: wilt not thou deliver my feet from falling, that I may walk before God in the light of the living?

Faced with problems of old age
Psalms 71

¹In thee, O LORD, do I put my trust: let me never be put to confusion.

²Deliver me in thy righteousness, and cause me to escape: incline thine ear unto me, and save me.

³Be thou my strong habitation, whereunto I may continually resort: thou hast given commandment to save me; for thou art my rock and my fortress.

⁴Deliver me, O my God, out of the hand of the wicked, out of the hand of the unrighteous and cruel man.

⁵For thou art my hope, O Lord GOD: thou art my trust from my youth.

⁶By thee have I been holden up from the womb: thou art he that took me out of my mother's bowels: my praise shall be continually of thee.

⁷I am as a wonder unto many; but thou art my strong refuge.

⁸Let my mouth be filled with thy praise and with thy honour all the day.

⁹Cast me not off in the time of old age; forsake me not when my strength faileth.

¹⁰For mine enemies speak against me; and they that lay wait for my soul take counsel together,

¹¹Saying, God hath forsaken him: persecute and take him; for there is none to deliver him.

¹²O God, be not far from me: O my God, make haste for my help.

¹³Let them be confounded and consumed that are adversaries to my soul; let them be covered with reproach and dishonour that seek my hurt.

¹⁴But I will hope continually, and will yet praise thee more and more.

¹⁵My mouth shall shew forth thy righteousness and thy salvation all the day; for I know not the numbers thereof.

¹⁶I will go in the strength of the Lord GOD: I will make mention of thy righteousness, even of thine only.

¹⁷O God, thou hast taught me from my youth: and hitherto have I declared thy wondrous works.

¹⁸Now also when I am old and greyheaded, O God, forsake me not; until I have shewed thy strength unto this generation, and thy power to every one that is to come.

[19]Thy righteousness also, O God, is very high, who hast done great things: O God, who is like unto thee!

[20]Thou, which hast shewed me great and sore troubles, shalt quicken me again, and shalt bring me up again from the depths of the earth.

[21]Thou shalt increase my greatness, and comfort me on every side.

[22]I will also praise thee with the psaltery, even thy truth, O my God: unto thee will I sing with the harp, O thou Holy One of Israel.

[23]My lips shall greatly rejoice when I sing unto thee; and my soul, which thou hast redeemed.

[24]My tongue also shall talk of thy righteousness all the day long: for they are confounded, for they are brought unto shame, that seek my hurt.

Dealing with Enemies
Nehemiah 4:4,5

[4]Hear, O our God; for we are despised: and turn their reproach upon their own head, and give them for a prey in the land of captivity:

[5]And cover not their iniquity, and let not their sin be blotted out from before thee: for they have provoked thee to anger before the builders

Lord it is nothing with thee to help, whether with many, or with them that have no power: help us, O Lord our God!

Prayer for a faithless people
Numbers 14:13-19

[13] But Moses objected. "What will the Egyptians think when they hear about it?" he asked the Lord. "They know full well the power you displayed in rescuing your people from Egypt. 14 Now if you destroy them, the Egyptians will send a report to the inhabitants of this land, who have already heard that you live among your people. They know, Lord, that

you have appeared to your people face to face and that your pillar of cloud hovers over them. They know that you go before them in the pillar of cloud by day and the pillar of fire by night. 15 Now if you slaughter all these people with a single blow, the nations that have heard of your fame will say, 16 'The Lord was not able to bring them into the land he swore to give them, so he killed them in the wilderness.'

17 "Please, Lord, prove that your power is as great as you have claimed. For you said, 18 'The Lord is slow to anger and filled with unfailing love, forgiving every kind of sin and rebellion. But he does not excuse the guilty. He lays the sins of the parents upon their children; the entire family is affected—even children in the third and fourth generations.' 19 In keeping with your magnificent, unfailing love, please pardon the sins of this people, just as you have forgiven them ever since they left Egypt."

God's dealings with enemies
Nehemiah 4:4,5

4Hear, O our God; for we are despised: and turn their reproach upon their own head, and give them for a prey in the land of captivity:

5And cover not their iniquity, and let not their sin be blotted out from before thee: for they have provoked thee to anger before the builders.

Safety

Job 5:11 he [1 Sam 2:7; Psalm 113:7] sets on high those who are lowly, and those who mourn are lifted to **safety**.

Psalm 4:8 In peace I will both [Psalm 3:5] lie down and sleep;for you alone, O LORD, make me [Psalm 16:9; Lev 25:18, 19; 26:5; Deut 33:28] dwell in **safety**.

Psalm 12:5 "Because [Psalm 9:12] the poor are plundered, because the needy groan, Isa 33:10; Psalm 82:8 I will now arise, says the LORD; I will place him in the [Psalm 55:18] **safety** for which he longs."

Ruby W. Smith, B.S., M.S., N.D.

Psalm 55:18 He redeems my soul in **safety** from the battle that I wage, for [Psalm 56:2] many are arrayed against me.

Psalm 78:53 [Exodus 14:19, 20] He led them in **safety**, so that they [Exodus 14:13] were not afraid, but [Exodus 14:27, 28; 15:10] the sea overwhelmed their enemies.

Proverbs 11:14 Where there is [Proverbs 15:22; 20:18; 24:6] no guidance, a people falls, but in an abundance of counselors there is **safety**.

Isaiah 10:31 Madmenah is in flight; the inhabitants of Gebim flee for **safety**.

Isaiah 14:30 And the firstborn of [Isaiah 29:19; Zeph 3:12] the poor will graze, and the needy lie down in **safety**; but I will kill your root with famine, and your remnant it will slay.

Isaiah 38:14

Jeremiah 8:7 a swallow or a crane I chirp;

Isaiah 59:11 I moan like a dove.

Psalm 69:3 My eyes are weary with looking upward. O Lord, I am oppressed;

Psalm 119:122;

Psalm 86:17;

Hebrew 7:22 be my pledge of **safety**!

Jeremiah 4:6 [Jeremiah 50:2; 51:12, 27] Raise a standard toward Zion, flee for **safety**, stay not, for I bring disaster from [Jeremiah 1:13] the north, [Isa 1:28] and great destruction.

Jeremiah 6:1 Flee for **safety**, Judg 1:21 O people of Benjamin,from the midst of Jerusalem!Blow the trumpet in [2 Sam 14:2 Tekoa,and raise a signal on

Neh 3:14 Beth-haccherem, for disaster looms Jeremiah 1:14 out of the north, and great destruction.

When dedicating to the Lord
I Samuel 1:10,11

¹⁰And she was in bitterness of soul, and prayed unto the LORD, and wept sore.

¹¹And she vowed a vow, and said, O LORD of hosts, if thou wilt indeed look on the affliction of thine handmaid, and remember me, and not forget thine handmaid, but wilt give unto thine handmaid a man child, then I will give him unto the LORD all the days of his life, and there shall no razor come upon his head.

Divine Mercy
Luke 18:13,14

¹³ And the publican, standing afar off, would not lift up so much as his eyes unto heaven, but smote upon his breast, saying, God be merciful to me a sinner.

¹⁴ I tell you, this man went down to his house justified rather than the other: for every one that exalteth himself shall be abased; and he that humbleth himself shall be exalted.

Offering

² Chronicles 35:8 And his officials contributed willingly to the people, to the priests, and to the Levites. [2 Chronicles 34:9, 14] Hilkiah, Zechariah, and Jehiel, the chief officers of the house of **God**, gave to the priests for the Passover **offering**s 2,600 Passover lambs and 300 bulls.

Ezra 1:4 And let each survivor, in whatever place he sojourns, be assisted by the men of his place with silver and gold, with goods and with beasts, besides freewill **offerings** for the house of **God** that is in Jerusalem."

Philippians 4:18 I have received full payment, and more. I am well supplied, [Philippians 2:25] having received from Epaphroditus the gifts you sent, [Gen 8:21] a fragrant **offering**,

Heb 13:16]a sacrifice acceptable and pleasing to **God** that is in Jerusalem."

Ezra 2:68 [Neh 7:70-72] Some of the heads of families, when they came to the house of the LORD that is in Jerusalem, made freewill **offerings** for the house of **God**, to erect it on its site.

Ezra 3:2 Then arose Jeshua the son of Jozadak, with his fellow priests, and [Matt 1:12; Luke 3:27

Zerubbabel the son of [1 Chr 3:17; Matt 1:12; Luke 3:27 Shealtiel with his kinsmen, and they built the altar of the **God** of Israel, to offer burnt **offerings** on it, Deut 12:5, 6]as it is written in the Law of Moses the man of **God**.

Deut 33:1

Ezra 6:9 And whatever is needed—bulls, rams, or sheep for burnt **offerings** to the **God** of heaven, wheat, salt, wine, or oil, as the priests at Jerusalem require—let that be given to them day by day without fail.

Printed in the United States
By Bookmasters